The Pol

The Parallels between the Presidencies of James K. Polk and Donald J. Trump

Alexandre G. Bojko

The Political Underdogs: The Parallels between the Presidencies of James K. Polk and Donald J. Trump
© 2020 by Alexandre G. Bojko
All Rights Reserved
Published by Alexandre G. Bojko
Haddonfield, NJ

No part of this publication may be reproduced, scanned, or transmitted in any form without written consent from the author.

Printed in the United States of America

ISBN: 978-1-7358996-9-5

Cover Design Images courtesy of the *Library of Congress* and the *National Portrait Gallery* in Washington D.C. All images in this book are in the Public Domain and may be used freely for commercial use.

To the Lord Jesus Christ Who gives me strength

Table of Contents

Introduction: The Political Enigma   1

Part 1: The Developmental Stages

1. The Shaping of Political Character   10

2. Men of Scholarly Pursuits   26

3. Mentors and Influences   39

4. The Beginning of Success   55

5. Spouses of Class   71

6. Rise to the Presidential Stage   80

7. The Common Man's Campaign   95

8. The Biased Press   106

9. The Day of Utmost importance   120

Part 2: The Influential Presidency

10. Americans in Disarray — 127

11. Presidencies of Nationalism — 139

12. A Change in Expectation and Pride — 179

13. Men of Equal Temperament — 187

14. Foreign Policy and Tensions with Mexico — 195

15. An Economic Revival — 239

16. Outcry from the Political Establishment — 261

17. Benefits for the Least Noticeable — 287

18. A National Rebirth — 296

Conclusion: Making America Great Again — 304

Introduction: The Political Enigma

On January 20, 2017, the nation witnessed the inauguration of Donald J. Trump, the forty-fifth president of the United States. People came from all over the country to gather in Washington, D.C., to view this historic moment, for it is not every day that a businessman, who has no political experience, takes the Oath of Office.

Following Trump's election, the public was divided. Ever since Trump announced his candidacy from Trump Tower in 2015, many Americans began to lose faith in the Republican Party. Many prominent Republicans in Congress believed that Trump would destroy the country. For instance, Lindsay Graham, a Republican senator from South Carolina, said in a tweet shortly after Trump won the Indiana primary, "If we nominate Trump, we will get destroyed . . . and we will deserve it."[1] Mitt Romney, the 2012

---

[1] Cillizza, Chris, and Aaron Blake. "The 10 Republicans who hate Donald Trump the most." The Washington Post. Last modified May 7, 2016.

Republican presidential nominee, accepted an endorsement from Trump when he was running for president against Democratic nominee Barack Obama. It was expected by many that Romney would return the favor and fully endorse the new Republican nominee. However, in the world of politics, self-interest can be more important than loyalty. Instead of supporting Trump, Romney attacked him, saying, "Donald Trump is a phony, a fraud. His promises are as worthless as a degree from Trump University. He's playing the American public for suckers: He gets a free ride to the White House, and all we get is a lousy hat."[2] Members of the opposing party went a step further with their insults; they began insulting Trump, calling him a racist, a bigot, and a womanizer. Additionally, shortly after Trump was elected, many Democrats created conspiracy theories that were later proven to be untrue, including that Trump colluded with the Russians to win the 2016 election.

---

[2] Cillizza, Chris. "Mitt Romney did Donald Trump a BIG favor by attacking him." The Washington Post. Last modified March 3, 2016.

Contrary to the opinions of many politicians in Washington, however, many Americans were attracted to the message of Donald J. Trump. Throughout his 2016 campaign, Trump held many rallies during which thousands of supporters flocked to hear him speak. Trump attracted people from all walks of life: the small business owner, the farmer from the Midwest, and the union worker, to name a few. In some ways, even though he was a wealthy businessman from New York, Trump campaigned for the common man. His famous campaign slogan, "Make America Great Again," was designed as a call to action to strengthen the United States and fix the problems many government officials in the nation's capital had chosen to avoid.

Trump was behind in almost every major poll leading up to the election, and many politicians and American citizens highly doubted that he would win. Hillary Clinton, the Democratic front-runner, said during the first presidential debate, "I think Donald just criticized me for preparing for this debate. And, yes, I did. You know what else I prepared for? I prepared to be president. And I think that's a good thing."[3] As the Democrats continued to hurl their insults at Trump, he retaliated and fought back against the party, which he believed cared only about benefiting their wealthy patrons.

As November approached, many Americans were looking forward to election day. The mainstream media, who thought they could convince the American people to vote for Clinton, berated Trump every time they had a chance. Their main goal was to convince what they thought was the gullible American public into voting for a Democratic candidate who, while many believed was corrupt, as evidenced by a low favorability rating, was an experienced politician. On November 8, 2016, the American people had a choice to make. They could vote for a businessman whose campaign was based on reviving the great American nation, or they could vote for a career politician. As the votes were being counted and Trump won the crucial swing

---

[3] Krieg, Gregory, and Daniella Diaz. "Clinton vs. Trump: The most memorable one-liners." CNN. Last modified September 27, 2016.

states of Pennsylvania, Florida, and Ohio, it was clear that he would be the next president. The mainstream media outlets began speaking words they thought would never be said: "We can now project that Donald Trump will be the forty-fifth president of the United States." Trump received 304 electoral votes to Clinton's 227. He was now the president-elect of the United States, and another president's title was added to the list of "dark horse" candidates.

Many adjectives are used to describe the atmosphere of the country after election day 2016. Supporters of Donald Trump were ecstatic that he had won the election and were looking forward to Inauguration Day and the grand reshaping of the American republic. Meanwhile, Clinton supporters were enraged that a businessman from New York had managed to beat the former Secretary of State. Tears were shed, protests were held, and property was destroyed, all as a result of the election of Donald J. Trump.

Many times, when decisions are made by the public that do not coincide with the elite establishment, the elite of the country will call on prominent historians to chastise the public on their severe mistakes in judgment. After Trump was inaugurated, Doris Kearns Goodwin, an American biographer, historian, and political commentator, said to Bill Maher on his weekly HBO talk show, "[Trump] has no humility which is an important part of every president; that he has no empathy; that he has no resilience . . . He says he's never experienced loss and that's why he has the very, very best temperament of anyone whose run . . . They can see that this is not a leader. This is not a man who has experienced any kind of empathy for other people."[4] David McCullough, the author of *1776* and *John Adams*, told *Time* magazine, "[Trump] said he does not read history, or presidential biographies, because, as he said, he has a mind that can reach beyond all that. That's utter nonsense. That's ego-centric illusion. To me, it's as if we've put someone in the pilot seat who has never flown a plane or even

---

[4] Schwartz, Ian. "Doris Kearns Goodwin: Persuade People to Dislike Trump." Real Clear Politics. Last modified October 6, 2018.

read about how you do it."[5]

Both historians and many American elitists believe that the 2016 election of Donald Trump to the office of the presidency showed a severe lack of judgment on the part of the American people. How could a businessman from New York who allegedly has no empathy and no public office experience become the forty-fifth president? How could someone like Donald Trump, who was berated by Democrats and even some Republicans, beat a former secretary of state and experienced politician? Many of these political pundits decry the election of President Trump as an epic fail of judgment of the American public. Many of these same pundits fail to delve into presidential history to analyze whether there had ever been a successful president who shared similar attributes to President Trump. In simplest terms: Have we ever had a President like this one before? Well, actually, we have.

---

[5] Waxman, Olivia B. "David McCullough: President Trump's Disregard for History Is 'Utter Nonsense.'" TIME. Last modified April 17, 2017.

His name was James Knox Polk. He was the eleventh president of the United States and served one term from 1845–1849. Polk was a man of the people, and he never allowed the opposition to derail him from his goals. Throughout his life, Polk was underestimated by many people. It was practically inconceivable that Polk was selected in May of 1844 as the Democratic Party nominee. He had not been successful in his reelection campaign for Governor of Tennessee, so how could he be successful in an even loftier endeavor? Even though Polk was a Democrat, the Democratic Party of 1844 was very different than the Democratic Party of today. The 19th-century Democratic Party was the party of the common man, the independent small-town farmer, and limited central authority. Polk, along with many other Democrats of the time, exemplified these ideals, and his policy goals benefited the majority of Americans, not a small percentage of the wealthy.

    Polk and Trump may have come from different parties; however, their early lives, presidential campaigns, administrative policies, press and media coverage, and interactions with the American public make them similar. The two of them are also one of the most complex pairs of political enigmas the nation has ever seen, and both perfectly exemplify what it means to be a political underdog.

Part 1:
The Developmental Stages

Chapter 1: The Shaping of Political Character

It is well-documented fact that people's early lives influence their future behavior. The lives of presidents are no exception. The challenges they face during their childhood impact their future policy-making decisions.

In the early 1700s, the United States experienced a rapid wave of immigration. These immigrants were different from the Puritans and Quakers, who left England to escape religious persecution. This new wave were mainly Presbyterian farmers who were strong-willed and earners of the title "workaholic."[6]

These immigrants were known as the Scots-Irish, and the Polk family was part of this migration wave. James K. Polk grew up in the same manner as the majority of Scots-Irish immigrants. He was born in a one-room log cabin

---

[6] Merry, Robert W. *A Country of Vast Designs: James K. Polk, the Mexican War, and the Conquest of the American Continent.* New York: Simon & Schuster, 2009. 13.

THE SHAPING OF POLITICAL CHARACTER

in Mecklenburg County, North Carolina, on November 2, 1795 and grew up with a Presbyterian mother and a father who was an established land speculator and surveyor.[7] At a young age, James moved with his family to Maury County, Tennessee, located in the state's backcountry. James's father operated a successful farm. He was able to procure it by using a real estate method that was popular with many westward settlers in the 19th century. According to historian Robert W. Merry, "settlers would venture forth into a thinly populated area and accumulate vast expanses of cheap or free land and develop as much acreage as possible for farming. When land prices rose with the arrival of subsequent pioneers, they sold undeveloped areas at elevated rates and used the profit to develop the retained acreage further and perhaps also venture into other commercial enterprises."[8] This formula worked very well for

---

[7] Ibid., 15.

[8] Ibid.

the Polk family, and it reinforced the robust Polk work ethic.

As James K. Polk grew into adolescence, he contracted specific ailments that defined not just his childhood but also his politically resilient character. At 17, Polk was diagnosed with bladder stones, which brought excruciating pain upon the young man. As a result, he was not able to compete in the usual backcountry activities, such as hunting and riding, that boys his age took part in. Polk's father sent him to Danville, Kentucky, where he would undergo a surgery that today would be considered an act of torture. Surprisingly, the surgery was a success, and Polk managed to continue life as he had before. However, the surgery did leave him with one major complication; it had damaged the nerves that line the prostate, which dominates sexual functions. As a result, Polk was sterile and unable to have children. The painful surgery he endured, the bullying he had received because of his ailments, and the work ethic shown by his father for his farm, instilled into James K. Polk his keen sense of will and resilience that he exemplified during his future presidency.[9]

Now, let's shift the focus to Donald Trump. How similar was his upbringing to Polk's, and what values did Trump gain from events that happened during his childhood? In 1869, the Trump legacy officially began with the birth of Friedrich Trump in Kallstadt, a village located in southwestern Germany that was then part of the Kingdom of Bavaria.[10] The Trump family was doing well in Kallstadt; however, when Friedrich's father died in 1877 at the age of 48, the family went into severe debt as a result of his medical expenses. In an attempt to remedy this debt, the Trump children, with the exception of Friedrich, worked on the family vineyard, picking grapes to be made into wine sold to merchants and traders. Not knowing what to do

---

[9] "Episode 11 - James K. Polk | PRESIDENTIAL podcast |." Video. YouTube. Posted by The Washington Post, April 24, 2018.

[10] Blair, Gwenda. *The Trumps: Three Generations of Builders and a President.* New York: Simon & Schuster, 2015. 25-28.

with feeble Friedrich, Katherina Kober Trump, Friedrich Trump's mother, did what she thought was best for her son and sent him to nearby Frankenthal to work as a barber's apprentice.[11] After Friedrich completed his apprenticeship, he returned to Kallstadt and realized there was no way to earn a living in his hometown. He was also approaching the age of eligibility for enlistment in the Imperial German Army.

In 1885, 16-year-old Friedrich Trump did what many other people from Europe did before him: emigrate to the United States to pursue the great American Dream. On October 17, his ship, the *SS Eider*, arrived at the Castle Garden Emigrant Landing Depot in New York City. Shortly after deboarding, Friedrich was fortunate enough to meet a German-speaking barber who was looking for an employee. As fate would have it, young Friedrich started working the next day. He lived on the Lower East Side of Manhattan. In 1891, he moved to Seattle, Washington.[12] With $600 in his

---

[11] Ibid., 29-30.

[12] Ibid., 41.

pocket, Trump bought the Poodle Dog restaurant, renamed it the Dairy Restaurant, and supplied it with new furnishings and fixtures. The Dairy Restaurant was in an area where sex and booze ran rampant, and the only form of entertainment was found in saloons, casinos, and brothels.[13] As a result of Friedrich's gung-ho spirit and work ethic, The Dairy Restaurant was a success, and it became the hotbed of action in Seattle. A year after settling in Seattle, Friedrich heard that gold and silver were being mined in Monte Cristo, Washington. Eager to capitalize on this opportunity, Friedrich sold the Dairy Restaurant and began the long journey to Monte Cristo.

Before leaving, however, Friedrich bought 40 acres in the Pine Lake Plateau, 12 miles east of Seattle, for $200. It was on this land that he would build a hotel. Because Friedrich could not afford to pay the full price for the land, he filed a Gold placer claim, which allowed him to claim exclusive mineral rights to the property without

---

[13] Speidel, Bill. *Sons of the Profits, Or, There's No Business like Grow Business: The Seattle Story, 1851-1901.* Seattle: Nettle Creek Pub., 1967. 291.

payment. However, there was one caveat: Friedrich could not build any structure on the land. This important point escaped his mind as he quickly bought lumber and constructed a hotel for the miners who thought they could strike it rich.[14]

Many miners felt confident that they would be able to get rich by finding gold; however, as with every "get rich quick" scheme, the miners soon discovered that few deposits of gold and even silver could be mined. As a result, many of the miners left the area, and Friedrich suffered from reduced business and a shortage of workers. While many people would have just given up at that moment, Friedrich Trump did not. In July 1897, news reached Monte Cristo that more than $700,000 worth of gold nuggets was found in the Klondike River, 1,200 miles north of Seattle.[15] By early 1898, Friedrich had enough money to pursue business opportunities in the Klondike located in northwestern Canada's Yukon

---

[14] Blair, *The Trumps*, Ibid., 61.

[15] Ibid., 73.

territory.

While traveling on the White Pass route to the Klondike, Friedrich couldn't help but notice the sheer amount of dead horses littered about. Capitalizing on this opportunity, he and a miner named Ernest Levin opened a tent restaurant along the route. They served delicacies of the Yukon, such as fresh-slaughtered horse meat, sourdough biscuits, and pancakes.[16] In May 1898, he and Levin traveled to Bennett, British Columbia, where they opened the two-story Arctic Restaurant and Hotel.[17] The Arctic Restaurant was known as one of the most extravagant restaurants, offering fresh fruit and a variety of meats and fishes. It became a big hit in the Klondike region.

In 1900, a railroad between Skagway, Alaska, and Whitehorse, located north of the Yukon River, was constructed and became fully operational. As a result, miners no longer had to

---

[16] Ibid., 84-85.

[17] Blair, Gwenda. "The Man Who Made Trump Who He Is." Politico. Last modified August 25, 2015.

endure the frigid conditions of the mountains and tundra. Attempting to profit from this opportunity, Friedrich relocated and literally floated the Arctic Restaurant to Whitehorse, the center of the new railroad terminal. The Arctic Restaurant experienced a massive revitalization when it came to Whitehorse, with its large steel ranges and chefs that could prepare 3,000 meals per day.[18] Amidst all these financial successes, however, Friedrich was about to be dealt a disappointing blow. Ernest Levin, Friedrich's business partner who had been by his side since the spring of 1898, broke up their business relationship in February 1901 due to Levin's drinking problem. They reconciled after two months, but their reconciliation was short-lived. Around that time, Major Zachary Taylor Wood, the great-grandson of Major General Zachary Taylor and assistant commissioner of the North-West Mounted Police, announced the prohibition of prostitution, gambling, and liquor. Fearing their economic downfall, Friedrich, along with

---

[18] Blair, *The Trumps*, 90.

other hotel and restaurant owners, petitioned the Canadian government and managed to postpone the enactment date from March 16 to June 1, 1901.[19] Fearing the worst, Friedrich sold his share of the restaurant to Levin and left Whitehorse. A few months later, the Canadian Mounties arrested Levin because of his drinking and seized custody of the Arctic Restaurant.[20]

Friedrich Trump managed to avoid and minimize his financial setbacks. His work ethic, keen business insights, and strong will to excel made him a successful person. These values became common characteristics among the Trump family.

Friedrich returned to Kallstadt in 1901 a wealthy man. He later met and proposed to Elizabeth Christ. His mother, however, disapproved of Elizabeth due to her lower social standing. Despite this, Friedrich Trump married Elizabeth Christ on August 26, 1902 and moved back to New York City, and the two of them lived

---

[19] Ibid., 91.

[20] Ibid., 93.

at 1006 Westchester Avenue in the predominately German-speaking neighborhood of Morrisania.[21] In 1904, Elizabeth gave birth to their daughter, also named Elizabeth. Soon after, Friedrich's wife became homesick and wanted to return to Germany, which they did later that year. Shortly after the family arrived in Germany, Bavarian authorities accused Friedrich Trump of avoiding conscription into the Imperial German Army. Therefore, he was considered a draft dodger. On December 24, 1904, the Department of Interior called for an investigation to strip Friedrich Trump of his German citizenship. From the investigation, they found that Friedrich had violated the Resolution of the Royal Ministry of the Interior number 9916, an 1886 law decreeing that "Those who left to avoid the army would be stripped of their citizenship and expelled."[22] No matter how hard Trump pleaded with the German government, he made no headway in maintaining

---

[21] Ibid., 96-97.

[22] Ibid., 99.

his citizenship.[23]

Ultimately, Friedrich and his family were stripped of their German citizenship and moved back to New York on June 30, 1905. In October of that year, their son Fred Trump, who would become the father of the forty-fifth president of the United States, was born. Friedrich Trump sold real estate in Queens until his death in May 1918 from the Spanish flu epidemic. His net worth was $31,359 when he passed away ($528,831 in current U.S. dollars).[24] Young Fred continued in his father's footsteps and became a prominent real estate developer in New York City in the borough of Queens. In 1923, Fred graduated from Richmond Hill High School in Queens and knew what he wanted to be: a house builder.

To gather more insights into the practice of home-building, Fred took night classes in carpentry at the local YMCA; he also studied

---

[23] Ibid., 100.

[24] Ibid., 118.

plumbing, masonry, and electrical wiring.[25] He was fascinated by construction, and he built his first house in Woodhaven, Queens, when he was still a teenager. Because Fred was under 21 years of age, his mother, Elizabeth, financed his houses and incorporated the business as "Elizabeth Trump & Son." As time went on, Fred's houses would be scattered all over Queens. In the 1930s, he created one of the first modern supermarkets in Woodhaven, and it quickly became popular. However, what could have been a new career for Fred was seen by him as a hinderance. As journalist and author Gwenda Blair remarks, "He wanted to build, not manage."[26] After six months, Fred Trump sold his supermarket to pursue his primary passion.

On January 11, 1936, Fred would marry the love of his life, Mary Anne Macleod, at the Carlyle Hotel.[27] They later moved to Jamaica,

---

[25] Ibid., 119.

[26] Interview with Robert Trump and John Walter, 2/16/95, quoted from *The Trumps*. 124.

[27] Ibid., 147-148.

Queens, and had five children: Maryanne Trump Barry, Fred Trump Jr., Elizabeth Trump Grau, Donald Trump, and Robert Trump.[28]

Fred Trump continued to display the Trump character traits of a strong work ethic and discipline. Although he was a family man, he held a reputation of being strict and authoritative. He enforced rigid curfews and had no tolerance for swearing or snacking before a meal. Every day when he came home from work, he would receive a report from Mary on the children's behavior and, based on that report, would act accordingly.[29] According to friends of the Trump children, punishments could range from being grounded for a couple days to being paddled with a wooden spoon. Even though Fred's parenting was aggressive, this style proved very useful, for it gave his children, especially Donald, the discipline and commitment to perform the task at hand.

---

[28] Powell, Kimberly. "Donald Trump's Family Tree." ThoughtCo. Last modified October 2, 2019.

[29] Blair, *The Trumps*, 228.

Fred Trump had a deep commitment to his country and cared about the American people. After World War II, more than six million soldiers, most of them young men, had come home to begin their civilian lives and found an unprecedented housing shortage.[30] In response, Fred promptly built a number of garden apartments and houses in Brooklyn and Queens that America's military personnel could easily afford.

Fred Trump continued to be a man of the people until his death of pneumonia in June 1999. Donald Trump was someone who took after his father. He was hardworking, dedicated, and had a strong sense of purpose. He was also not a person to back down from a fight, even in his early years. He was raised in the Presbyterian religion, but many say he has never asked God for forgiveness, believing "If I do something wrong, I just try and make it right. I don't bring God into that picture."[31]

---

[30] U.S. Census Bureau and Washington Post, 8/16/54.

[31] Scott, Eugene. "Trump believes in God, but hasn't sought forgiveness." CNN. Last modified July 18, 2015.

THE SHAPING OF POLITICAL CHARACTER

James K. Polk's and Donald Trump's respective childhoods had a profound impact on their adult lives. When we study their respective presidencies, it is evident that the values they learned from their parents are present in how they managed their lives and ultimately ran their administrations.

Chapter 2: Men of Scholarly Pursuits

Every child in the United States of America is legally required to attend school until the age of 16 (and in some states, 18). Some people enjoy school, while others do not. Some excel in their classes, and others do not fare as well. If there is one character trait that education can instill into the minds of successful people, it is the concept of being dedicated and a hard worker. These character traits were demonstrated within both Presidents James K. Polk and Donald J. Trump by the way they conducted themselves in office, through their commitments and kept promises, and the policies they passed. Both presidents also exemplified the characteristic of hard work tirelessly, dedicating themselves to act in the best interests of the American people.

When an average person looks at James K. Polk's background, they believe that he was uneducated. After all, he grew up in the Tennessee backcountry, where the main issues of importance were farming and keeping your family safe from neighboring American Indian tribes. In reality, Polk was far from uneducated. Shortly after his gruesome surgery, he resumed his formal schooling with diligence and enthusiasm. As Eugene Irving McCormac remarked in his biography on the eleventh president, Polk proved to be "diligent in his studies, and his moral conduct was exceptional and exemplary."[32] The same author later describes Polk as displaying "literary merit and moral worth" at Bradley Academy in Murfreesboro.[33] Upon being granted admission into the University of North Carolina, Polk graduated at the top of his class with impressive accomplishments in both mathematics and classics.[34]

It was at the University of North Carolina where Polk started to develop himself. Here, Polk

---

[32] McCormac, Eugene Irving. *James K. Polk: A Political Biography*. Newtown, Conn.: American Political Biography Press, 1995.3.

[33] Ibid.

[34] Merry, *Vast Designs,* 16.

developed the values he would prioritize as president. Polk never considered himself brilliant and knew he lacked character traits possessed by other students in his graduating class. Yet, he soon realized his true capabilities rested in his unwavering diligence and work ethic. Even historian Robert W. Merry remarks, "[Polk] acquired a seriousness of purpose and intensity of ambition that would become hallmark traits."[35] When you look at Polk's moral conscience, it is evident why he didn't drink, why he had no sense of humor, and why he didn't participate in frivolous activities of the time, such as going to the theater or listening to an opera.[36] Polk was different than many other people of his time; however, it is the seriousness and unwavering diligence with which he approached the task at hand that propelled him to the vital role of president of the United States.

Donald Trump's educational experience, while similar in some ways to Polk's, was

---

[35] Ibid.

[36] Ibid. "James K. Polk | PRESIDENTIAL podcast |"

notably different. In his pre-teen years, Trump attended the Kew-Forest School in Forest Hills, Queens. If one were to guess how well Trump performed in his studies at this school, they would likely think he excelled there. After all, he came from a prominent family; therefore, he had to excel. Unfortunately, that was not the case. During the 2016 election, mainstream media outlets were digging deep to find evidence of Donald Trump's supposed troubled childhood. One news article labeled schoolboy Trump as being, "A classroom know-it-all who could never admit he was wrong and boasted of giving his music teacher a black eye. He was also a show-off who yearned to hear the crowd's applause . . . but who would smash his baseball bat in fury if he didn't win."[37]

After hearing these accusations, how could one find similarities between the respective educational journeys of Donald Trump and James K. Polk? Trump was not at the top of his

---

[37] Jefferson, Andrea. "Biographer Reveals Trump Was a Vicious Bully as a Child Who Threw Rocks at Babies." Political Flare. Last modified October 4, 2019.

class like Polk, and he certainly did not possess qualities of "literary merit."[38] From the start of his educational career, Trump was not a well-rounded student like Polk, and he certainly was neither interested in politics nor a skilled debater. So, when did Trump's academic life start to change?

Well, it all started when Trump transferred from the Kew-Forest School at the age of 13 to the New York Military Academy. Fred Trump and his wife, Mary Anne, believed that this would be the best option for Donald after some issues occurred at his old school. Donald would spend the next five years of his educational career at the New York Military Academy.

In the beginning, life at the academy did not go well for Trump. During his first year, he got into altercations with his fellow cadets and was not always keen on taking directives from his teachers.[39] However, while many people believed

---

[38] McCormac, *Polk*, 3.

[39] Mcintosh, Sandy. "How young Donald Trump was slapped and punched until he made his bed." New York Daily News. Last modified August 11, 2017.

that Trump would fail at the Military Academy, he actually excelled. According to a recent report written by *EDU In Review*, "[Trump] earned many academic honors, was a member of the varsity football team in 1962, the varsity soccer team in 1963, and the varsity baseball team from 1962-1964."[40] By his senior year, Trump was thriving under the rigorous curriculum and social life of the New York Military Academy.[41]

When it came time for college, Trump had an important decision to make on what to study. Ultimately, he decided to major in business. Originally, he attended Fordham University, but he soon realized that he needed to test himself against the best students in order to succeed.[42] The college which Trump believed had the best students was the Wharton School of Finance in Pennsylvania, one of the leading business schools

---

[40] "Donald Trump's Education Background." EDUInReview.com.

[41] Ibid.

[42] Trump, Donald, and Tony Schwartz. *Trump: The Art of the Deal*. New York: Random House, 1988. 46.

in the United States. While Trump attended Wharton, he learned the business skills needed to be a successful real estate developer. In 1968, Trump graduated from Wharton with a bachelor's degree in economics.

Graduating from Wharton was an important accomplishment for Donald Trump. In a 2015 "Meet the Press" interview, Trump described Wharton as "probably the hardest there is to get into," adding, "Some of the great business minds in the world have gone to Wharton."[43] Although Trump emerged from Wharton a famous real estate mogul, he hadn't made many strong connections with the other students, and he even dismissed the significance of his degree.[44] As Trump wrote in *The Art of the Deal*, "In my opinion, that [Wharton] degree doesn't prove very much, but a lot of people I do business with take it very seriously, and it's considered very

---

[43] Spinelli, Dan. "Trump flaunts Wharton degree, but his college years remain a mystery." The Daily Pennsylvanian. Last modified August 19, 2015

[44] Ibid.

prestigious." He continues, explaining, "It didn't take long to realize that there was nothing particularly awesome or exceptional about my classmates, and that I could compete with them just fine."[45]

When it came to Trump's grades at Wharton, reports vary. Some say he was at the top of his class, while others say he focused more on his business ventures than his academics.[46] Most of the time, Trump was barely seen on campus, and while this automatically led to some students speculating about his intelligence, he was actually refining his passion for business and real estate development in New York City.

Although the majority of Trump's classmates believed Trump was an average student not meant for Wharton, other classmates liked the future real estate mogul. Ted Sachs was one such classmate, and he had a different view of Trump. Sachs believed that "Trump was a really nice

---

[45] Trump, Tony *et al. The Art of the Deal*. 46.

[46] Ibid., "Trump flaunts Wharton degree"

low-key guy; he was very self-effacing, and he never talked about himself."[47] Although Sachs and Trump were good friends throughout their time at Wharton, their friendship started to become less and less meaningful after Trump's level of fame increased. Sachs articulates in one interview, "I was lost—I didn't get it, I thought he kept two sides to his life, as some people are capable of doing."[48] When Trump emerged as the Republican presidential candidate in the 2016 election, Sachs said he was not surprised and explained that Trump "Had a magnetism about himself. He knew where he was going—that was clear."[49] He closed with this important message: "I suspect underneath there's a decent guy. Fifty years is a long time. After any relationship, does anyone really know a person?"[50]

With all the facts presented above, the question

---

[47] Ibid.

[48] Ibid.

[49] Ibid.

[50] Ibid.

still remains: What values did Donald Trump gain from his schooling, and how are these values similar to the ones Polk gained? One of the most important values that both men developed prior to their respective presidencies was a sense of seriousness. Many people would agree that Polk, who had endured a childhood full of pain and graduated at the top of his class at the University of North Carolina, had a sense of seriousness, but it is often wondered how Trump could also have this sense. After all, from the onset, it didn't appear that Trump cared about his academic standing. Trump acquired his sense of seriousness after his admission into the Wharton School of Finance. It was there that Trump finally decided he was going to be the best among the rest. To achieve that goal, he needed to be serious and to not involve himself in frivolous activities. This was one of the main reasons Trump was rarely seen on campus; he was focusing on bettering himself so that he could be the best and continue in his father's footsteps.

The other value that both Trump and Polk had was a strong work ethic. Polk would not have been the best in his class or a skilled debater if he had not worked hard. He was someone who worked harder than anyone else because he was not born smart; thus, he needed to be diligent in his studies to succeed. As time went on, he would use his work ethic to become a prominent political figure in Tennessee before attaining the title of eleventh president of the United States. Donald Trump is no different. Even though he came from an affluent family and had access to opportunities that James K. Polk could have only dreamed about, he still had to work hard to get somewhere in his life. If Trump had continued to act in the same way that he did at the Kew-Forest School, he would not have been successful. A significant change in temperament and character had to occur. That change occurred at Wharton, for if he had continued to attend Fordham University instead of transferring to Wharton, he would not have known the true definition of what it means to excel against the best.

Polk and Trump, though they had very different educational experiences, acquired the same values. They learned the values of hard work and commitment, which proved beneficial in their respective adulthoods. After college, Polk would become the Speaker of the House from 1835–1839 and later Governor of Tennessee from 1839–1841; he would then partake in one of the most daring adventures of his political career when he ran for president in 1844 and successfully defeated the Whig candidate, Henry Clay. Trump, although not yet an aspiring politician, would take over his father's real estate business and become one of the most successful real estate moguls in the country. He would then go on to create the popular NBC TV show *The Apprentice,* where he would coin his famous phrase, "You're fired!" Finally, in 2015, he would announce his run for president from Trump Tower and participate in one of the most dramatic elections in modern-day America, the election of 2016. Trump would ignore his critics and prove all the politicians wrong by beating a well-seasoned and established Democratic figure. He would later secure the presidency and take the Oath of Office to become the forty-fifth president of the United States.

Historian Robert W. Merry, the author of a comprehensive book on Polk's presidency titled *A Country of Vast Designs*, points out, "[Polk] carried himself with a dignity and self-confidence that led many to see him eventually as a man of mark."[51] This quote is also relevant today, for Donald Trump also had a degree of self-confidence that made him stand out from the crowd.

---

[51] Merry, *Vast Designs*, 17.

Chapter 3: Mentors and Influences

The Information Revolution has given people the opportunity to follow someone they admire. In a world where celebrities and world-class athletes are highly regarded, people often go to great lengths to follow their daily lives on social media. The majority of "followers" never meet their idols, but there are those rare cases where they not only meet, but their idol becomes their mentor. When it comes to the mentors of future presidents, it is important to remember that the student will often take on some of the characteristics of the teacher. To understand the behavior of presidents, it is helpful to study the values and attributes of their mentors.

If you were to ask the majority of historians for the one person in James K. Polk's life who influenced him the most, they would probably answer Andrew Jackson, the seventh president of the United States. Andrew Jackson grew up in poverty in the Carolinas but ultimately managed to become a wealthy Tennessee lawyer. He became a national hero after his victory at the

Battle of New Orleans during the War of 1812. He was an advocate for minimal centralized government power and campaigned on the idea of expanding voting rights to the common man and the masses. He eventually rose to the office of president and became the leader of the newly formed Democratic Party. [52]

Jackson's childhood was not typical of an aspiring future politician. Born on March 15, 1767 in the Waxhaw region of the Carolinas, Jackson grew up in poverty. His family was too busy trying to make ends meet to care for their child; therefore, Jackson needed to develop self-reliance at a young age.[53] In his adolescent years, Jackson became brash and combative, for he was seen as the main protector and caretaker of his family. As with most backcountry settlers, Jackson did not have a formal education, which would become a subject of ridicule when he eventually rose up in the political ranks. He

---

[52] Editors History. "Andrew Jackson." History. Last modified October 29, 2009.

[53] Merry, *Vast Designs,* 19.

MENTORS AND INFLUENCES

studied law on his own and was admitted to the bar in 1787. At the age of 21, Jackson moved to Tennessee, where he practiced law, acquired property, and enlisted in the Tennessee militia.[54]

In 1796, Jackson became Tennessee's first congressman and served one term as senator. It was during those times when the pioneer population was increasing and the Native American threat was looming that Jackson thrived and led the Tennessee militia into battle. Jackson's combative and brash nature made him a desirable leader among his men, and he continued to excel in the military. In 1814, Major General Jackson would lead the Americans to victory in the Battle of Horseshoe Bend. A year later, he would become a national hero after he defeated the British at the Battle of New Orleans. Three years later, he attacked the Seminole Indians in Spanish Florida. When news of Jackson's military exploits reached Washington, President Monroe, as well as members of his cabinet, were furious that Jackson had not taken

---

[54] Ibid., 20.

a more diplomatic approach with the Seminole Indians. Ironically, John Quincy Adams, Monroe's secretary of state, applauded the Major General's military campaign and demanded that Spain cede the Florida territory to the United States. In 1819, Adams negotiated the Florida Purchase Treaty in which the United States officially acquired Florida from Spain. On March 10, 1821, Monroe appointed Jackson to take possession of Florida and gave him the full power of Governor. This action further propelled Andrew Jackson to the national stage, and by the 1820s, he was one of the country's most glorified figures. However, he was not without his controversies.[55]

Andrew Jackson had risen from his life of poverty to become a national hero. During this time, he had acquired values such as determination, toughness, and a strong will. These would prove useful in the future. In 1825, while Jackson was in his heyday, the young James K. Polk arrived in Washington, D.C. After

---

[55] Ibid., 21-22.

serving in the Tennessee State Legislature, Polk decided to run for Congress. With the endorsement of Jackson, Polk's future presidential mentor, Polk won the congressional seat and headed to Washington. This was not the first time that Jackson had helped Polk. Frequently, Polk asked Jackson questions on how to pursue his political goals and aspirations. Jackson remarked that in order to become an experienced politician, Polk needed to find a wife that was of high status and, most importantly, knew the ins and outs of the America's political scene.[56] Taking Jackson's advice, Polk married Sarah Childress, a member of a prominent Tennessean family whose knowledge of politics was nothing short of exemplary, on New Year's Day, 1824.

One year prior to Polk's arrival in Washington, the nation's capital had been through a rough time. The election of 1824 was controversial. Four candidates were running for the presidency: Andrew Jackson, John Quincy Adams, Henry

---

[56] Ibid., 17.

Clay, and William Crawford. All of the candidates were Democratic-Republicans, but they each had different views on the role of government in people's lives. The results of the election were as follows: Jackson received 154,000 votes, Adams 109,000, and Clay and Crawford each had around 47,000. In the Electoral College, Jackson received 99 votes, Adams 84 votes, Crawford 41 votes, and Clay 37 votes.[57] Although Jackson received the most electoral votes, none of the candidates received an electoral majority. Thus, the House of Representatives was tasked with choosing a president out of a choice of three. Henry Clay was automatically out because he had come in fourth, and William Crawford was not healthy, for he had recently had a paralytic stroke. The two remaining choices were Jackson and Adams. Henry Clay, though out of the race, could influence the outcome of the election, for he was speaker of the House. On February 9, 1825, the

---

[57] Nelson, Michael. *Guide to the Presidency*. 2nd ed. Washington, DC: Congressional Quarterly, 1996. 1406; Merry, *Vast Designs*, 25.

House held its election, in which each state delegation got one vote. Before the House voted, it was rumored that several back-room talks had been conducted between Adams and the speaker of the House regarding the potential outcomes of the upcoming vote. Although these talks did occur, the subject of them remains unknown. However, one thing was for certain: Clay had announced publicly that he supported Adams, and because of his influential position as speaker, John Quincy Adams became the sixth president of the United States.[58] In return for his support, Adams made Clay secretary of state. This action angered many of Jackson's supporters, and they denounced the outcome as a corrupt bargain.

While this "corrupt bargain" angered many Jackson supporters, it made Jackson's campaign in the next election even more retributive. Jackson, enraged by the results of the election, would take any opportunity he had to destroy the

---

[58] McNamara, Robert. "The Election of 1824 Was Decided in the House of Representatives." ThoughtCo. Last modified September 23, 2019.

credibly of the recently elected Adams administration.[59]

Amidst all of the turmoil in Washington, James K. Polk stepped into action. On March 13, 1826, he delivered his maiden floor speech to the House, proposing a constitutional amendment stating that future presidents were to be elected by the people, not a legislative body like the House of Representatives. This point echoed the ideals of Jacksonian democracy, where the common man, not just the aristocrats, had a say. To support his argument, Polk used essential founding documents such as the preamble of the Constitution and the Federalist Papers.[60] Polk would later win reelection to the House in 1827. In the same year, the Jacksonian Democrats took control of the House. Polk viewed the Democratic majority in the House as ". . . a great

---

[59] Merry, *Vast Designs,* 26.

[60] Polk, James K. "On the proposition to amend the Constitution of the United States, respecting the election of president and vice president." Speech, The House of Representatives, Washington, DC, March 13, 1826.

triumph."[61]

As the 1828 election was fast approaching, Jackson's closest supporters were developing their campaign rhetoric against the Adams administration, and Polk saw this opportunity as a way to learn the political tactics of his mentor. He joined the Nashville Central Committee; a pro-Jackson operation set up to counter any campaign allegations against Jackson. In the upcoming election, there would be many accusations against Jackson, including murder, adultery, dueling, gambling, drinking, cockfighting, and swearing. Henry Clay, who had an intense hatred of Jackson, attempted to defame Jackson's heroic image by bringing forth all of his past indiscretions to the public. A notable example was the Coffin Handbills, which framed Jackson as a cold-blooded killer during his many

---

[61] Polk, James K., Herbert Weaver, Paul H. Bergeron, Wayne Cutler, Tom Chaffin, and Michael David Cohen. *Correspondence of James K. Polk*. Nashville: Vanderbilt University Press, 1968. 100.

military exploits.[62]

Despite these allegations, the campaign of Jackson's redemption was in full swing. When studying the election of 1828, it is essential to point out a dramatic shift that had taken place just prior to this time. Before the election, the only Americans who had the right to vote were wealthy, white elitists who owned property and paid taxes. When it came to electing a government official such as the president, the congressional caucus was used. This was a process where the elites of a political party would choose their candidate, and the public would be barred from interfering in this important decision. By the late 1820s, a shift from an elitist democracy to a common man democracy had occurred. With property rights for voting reduced and public nominating conventions being implemented, the true meaning of American democracy that we know of today was taking form. As a result, a new mass electorate was created, and, in order to win this crucial election,

---

[62] Merry, *Vast Designs*, 27.

Jackson needed to garner their support. Based on his childhood experiences, this task would prove to be effortless for Jackson but difficult for the incumbent, John Quincy Adams.[63]

Jackson supporters used the words of their attackers against them to paint their candidate in a more favorable light. Along with the corrupt bargain from the election of 1824, they attacked John Quincy Adams' presidency. Many Jacksonians criticized Adams' large federal salaries he had received over the years. They even called Adams a pimp, accusing him of having sexual relations with a servant girl of the Russian Tsar during negotiations regarding the vital Russo-American treaty.[64] Adams' supporters, on the other hand, took their insults a step further. They called Andrew Jackson's mother a common prostitute, and his wife Rachel

---

[63] Ibid., 28.

[64] Kennedy, David M., Lizabeth Cohen, and Thomas Andrew Bailey. *The American Pageant: [Gr. 9-12]: A History of the Republic.* 12th ed. Boston, MA: Houghton Mifflin, 2002. 259.

a convicted adulteress. When Rachel died days after the election, Jackson entered a state of mourning that continued for the majority of his presidency. He blamed the verbal accusers for the death of his wife, even though she had actually died of a heart attack.

Despite all of the verbal abuse and hardships caused by Adams supporters, Jackson carried 56 percent of the popular vote to Adams's 43.6 percent; he also gained 178 electoral votes to Adams's 83.[65] In addition, Jacksonian Democrats swept both houses of Congress by significant margins, thus paving the way for their success in the coming years.

In the years that followed, Polk would learn from his mentor, and, using his knowledge of current political issues and his exceptional oratory skills, he would defend President Jackson from any and all accusations brought against him. As the struggle between Jackson and his political rivals intensified, Polk would further thrust

---

[65] Merry, *Vast Designs*, 29.

himself onto the national stage,[66] all the while looking up to his presidential mentor, Andrew Jackson. When Polk became president, he would behave in the same manner as Jackson and incorporate the character traits of grit, resilience, and strong will into his personality and governing style.

Unlike Polk, Donald Trump did not have a presidential mentor. He was influenced more by his father than anyone else. Since the Trump Organization was family-run, his father taught him the business. As he took over the real estate empire from his father, his circle of influence was expanded to include his business associates. One could argue that these interactions were more due to similarities in approach rather than influence. One such associate was Roy Cohn, an American lawyer. Cohn did not persuade Trump to run for the office of president, but Trump respected Cohn because he found in him a character trait that he possessed himself, which was never backing down from a fight.

---

[66] Ibid., 30.

Roy Cohn rose to national fame in the 1950s as a result of his involvement with the Second Red Scare. At the time, Joseph McCarthy, a U.S. senator from the state of Wisconsin, hired Cohn as his chief counsel, and they worked together on the Senate Permanent Subcommittee on Investigations related to the communist threat.[67] Roy Cohn was considered a protector of American democracy. Some people, however, had a negative opinion of Cohn, and at one point he was indicted on bribery, conspiracy, and bank fraud charges. Even though Cohn was put on trial for each of these allegations, he was acquitted all three times. While some believed Cohn was guilty, regardless of the court outcome, Donald Trump, at that point a Manhattan real estate mogul, was not one of them. Trump's personality fit well with Cohn's, as both men believed in fighting for what you believe and never

---

[67] *EXECUTIVE SESSIONS OF THE SENATE PERMANENT SUBCOMMITTEE ON INVESTIGATIONS OF THE COMMITTEE ON GOVERNMENT OPERATIONS.: Hearings on S. 84 Before the COMMITTEE ON GOVERNMENT OPERATIONS*, 83d Cong., 1st Sess. (1953).

compromising on your convictions.[68]

Cohn handled a number of cases for the Trump Organization. In each of them, he showed the same tenacity for defending his client as Trump showed in the defense of his positions. The cases in themselves are not important. What is important is that Trump surrounded himself with fighters.

When Trump began his campaign to run for the office of the president, the relationship he had had with Cohn during the 1970s and 1980s was again being examined. The people wondered how much of Cohn's behavior was present in the Republican presidential candidate. One could argue that Trump's resilience, hard work, and courage to never back down from a fight are probably what attracted him to Cohn. Others would argue that Cohn reinforced those characteristics.[69]

Presidential mentors are helpful but not

---

[68] Blair, The Trumps, 251.

[69] Kruse, Michael. "The Final Lesson Donald Trump Never Learned from Roy Cohn." Politico Magazine. Last modified September 19, 2019.

definitive in understanding how a president will behave under certain circumstances. Both Polk and Trump learned and reinforced the following life lessons from their mentors and business associates: Approach every problem with resilience and a fighting spirit, and never compromise on your integrity and convictions. Because the Trump Organization was a family-run business, Donald Trump was most influenced by his father. As Trump took over the business, he surrounded himself with people who had the same tenacity for defending their positions. Through their presidencies, both Polk and Trump would experience setbacks; however, because they were influenced by people who had overcome adversity, they received the training necessary to do the same.

Chapter 4: The Beginning of Success

Success is measured in different ways. It can mean being accepted to a prestigious university or getting the dream job you have always wanted. Sometimes, it means earning a raise or a promotion. Success can also mean achieving national prominence. In summary, success can be defined in an infinite number of ways.

To be successful, we must not allow setbacks to derail our goals and aspirations. Throughout American history, there have been many individuals who positively confronted setbacks in their lives. Abraham Lincoln, the 16th president of the United States who championed the elimination of slavery in the country and ultimately the ratification of the Thirteenth Amendment, lost his job at 23, the love of his life Ann Rutledge to typhoid at 26, and many congressional races. Despite these setbacks, Lincoln became the 16th president, tasked with keeping the Union together during the difficult

Civil War period; this made him one of America's most notable presidents.

Another notable historical figure who endured many setbacks was Thomas Edison, credited with such inventions as the light bulb, the automatic telegraph, the carbon telephone transmitter, the phonograph, the movie camera, and alkaline storage batteries. Edison was one of seven siblings in a large family, was homeschooled by his mother, and had a hard time hearing. Despite these setbacks and his lack of formal schooling, Edison prospered in life. In 1877, he invented the phonograph, an invention that earned him the title "The Wizard of Menlo Park." A year later, Edison began working on a commercially viable incandescent lightbulb.[70] He experimented with thousands of different filaments and struggled to find the filament that burned the longest. Although the light at the end of the tunnel seemed far away, Edison did not give up and worked hard to achieve his goal. He even coined a quote that

---

[70] "48 Famous Failures Who Will Inspire You To Achieve." Wanderlust Worker.

people still use to this day: "Genius is one percent inspiration and ninety-nine percent perspiration."[71]

These historical figures succeeded in life despite the obstacles they faced. Being successful requires not only intelligence but also hard work and resilience. Both Presidents Polk and Trump experienced failures in their lives, but they separated themselves from others by the way they handled these obstacles.

In the early 1830s, tensions were running high in Washington, D.C. The common man, composed of Western settlers and working-class citizens, hated the so-called elites, who advocated for stronger centralized power. Perhaps the most heated topic during the Jacksonian era was the constitutionality of the Second Bank of the United States.

The concept of a national bank was first proposed by Alexander Hamilton, who saw it as a federal institution designed to strengthen the emerging United States economy through the

---

[71] Northup, Cynthia Clark. *The American Economy: A Historical Encyclopedia.* ABC-CLIO, INC. 2003. 94.

management of federal loans and the stabilization of the nation's currency. Thomas Jefferson opposed chartering a national bank because the Constitution did not allow such an action to take place, and if a bank were chartered, an unhealthy alliance between the government and wealthy businessmen would be formed. Despite the negatives associated with having a national bank, the First Bank of the United States was chartered in 1791.

The First Bank of the United States, established in Philadelphia, would serve as the nation's financial center. Its charter expired in 1811, but its lifetime was extended due to the financial responsibilities of the War of 1812.[72] Five years later, the Second Bank of the United States was chartered and immediately slipped into corruption. The bank's president started to speculate in its stock, and when this led to increased debt, state banks were forced to redeem their loans and bank notes, resulting in an inflationary period. Furthermore, the risky

---

[72] Merry, *Vast Designs*, 35.

business of land speculation in the West resulted in loan defaults and, ultimately, bank failures. These factors lead to the dreadful Panic of 1819, a period of unemployment, poverty, and economic turmoil.[73]

When the question of the legality of the Second Bank of the United States was brought to the attention of Andrew Jackson, his response was not surprising. Jackson abhorred this concentration of economic power because of the negative economic effects it had on his supporters in the West.[74] Jackson did not hate all banks; rather, he hated monopolistic banks that acted in the interests of wealthy elitists rather than the American working class. This issue became a point of focus during the election of 1832. Nicholas Biddle, the bank's president, held an incredible amount of political influence. He maintained an extensive network of political friendships and created his own political party, in

---

[73] Ibid.

[74] Ibid., 36.

a way, made of pro-bank, wealthy congressmen and senators.[75] Henry Clay wanted to create a backlash during the crucial election year. In the summer of 1832, he asked Biddle to submit to Congress an early charter renewal of the Second Bank of the United States that was due to expire in 1836. Clay wanted to create a lose-lose situation for Jackson, who was running for reelection. If Jackson signed the charter, he would lose supporters in the West. If he vetoed the charter, he risked losing his reelection bid by alienating wealthy and influential groups in the East.[76]

When the pro-bank forces attacked Jackson, James K. Polk was there to defend the actions of his mentor. In the House of Representatives, Polk attacked the administrators of the Second Bank for requesting a re-charter and fought back against the politicians who had justified voting for it. Meanwhile, Jackson commissioned the

---

[75] Ibid.

[76] Kennedy, David M., et al. *The American Pageant*. 270-71.

House of Representatives' Committee on Ways and Means to conduct an investigation on the Bank's allegedly corrupt practices. The investigation found that the Bank was violating its charter by allowing foreigners to vote for directors, and they also found suspicious payments made to many prominent American politicians of the time. These investigations gave Jackson the confidence he needed to follow through with his veto.[77]

Despite the actions of pro-bank forces, Jackson won reelection in November with 219 electoral votes to Henry Clay's 49. Serving another term in office, Jackson vowed to destroy the Second Bank by withdrawing federal funds from its vaults and depositing them in various state banks, nicknamed "pet banks" because of their undying allegiance to the Democrats and Jackson. Polk continued to support Andrew Jackson when it came to the elimination of the

---

[77] Jimmy Polk, ed. "Andrew Jackson, James K. Polk, and The Panic of 1819." Jimmypolk.com. Last modified March 20, 2020.

Second Bank. As a result of his brilliant legislative success in the House, Polk emerged as somewhat of a national figure. Democratic newspapers such as *The Daily Globe* labeled Polk's oratory as "perfectly irresistible."[78] In 1835, Polk became Speaker of the House. Thomas Hart Benton, a senator from Missouri who would later support Polk's doctrine of Manifest Destiny, called his position "a test of the administration's strength, Mr. Polk being supported by that party."[79]

Although Polk's election as speaker was seen as a triumph in Washington, it was not viewed in the same way in his state of Tennessee, where the party affiliation had changed from Democrat to Whig. In 1836, another presidential election was held. Jackson did not run for a third term, maintaining, like presidents before him, the tradition of serving a maximum of two terms. He

---

[78] F.P. Blair. "Mr. Polk's Bank Report," *The Daily Globe*, March 6, 1833.

[79] Benton, Thomas Hart. *Thirty Years' View*. New York: D. Appleton, 1854. 569.

THE BEGINNING OF SUCCESS

fully supported vice-president Martin Van Buren, who ran for president under the Democratic Party. As a result of the national bank war, a new political party emerged known as the Whigs. The Whigs were described as an unorganized incompatibility; however, the main glue holding all of its members together was their hatred of Jackson.[80] The Whigs decided to run four candidates in the 1836 election to deny the majority of the electoral votes from being pledged to Van Buren, resulting in the election being forced to be decided in the House of Representatives. The candidates were: William Henry Harrison, Daniel Webster, Willie Person Mangum, and Hugh Lawson White. This plan did not succeed, and when the votes were counted in November, Van Buren won the election with 170 electoral votes. The Whigs' plan had backfired, but the results of this election changed the political makeup of some states.

Hugh Lawson White had managed to switch the once Democratic Tennessee to favor the

---

[80] Kennedy, David M., et al. *The American Pageant*. 272.

Whigs. White's Tennessee supporters, combined with the state's new Whig demographic, allowed the Whig Party to take root in the state, heavily influencing thousands of Tennesseans.[81] This drastic change hurt Polk in future gubernatorial elections.

While Jackson was president, he taught Democrats like Polk one essential value: Never backing down from a fight. Polk defended his colleagues as speaker of the House, amongst some insults from Whig politicians. He refused to respond to the insults, proving he was a man of discipline and character.

As political changes in Washington occurred, Polk adopted and embraced them. When his colleagues were being attacked, he responded to their attackers with brilliant oratory and intelligence. Polk did not allow the opinions of the opposition to deflect him from his goals. This trait made him successful not just in the House of Representatives but also as president.

Similarly, Donald Trump experienced many

---

[81] Merry, *Vast Designs,* 44.

challenges in the real estate business. Like Polk, he adapted to the changes and did not let the opinions of others jeopardize his success. Shortly after he graduated from the Wharton School of Finance, he returned to New York and took over his father's lucrative real estate company in 1971. Shortly after this, he changed its focus. Elizabeth Trump & Son, which initially focused on building and renting apartments in Brooklyn, Queens, and Staten Island, was branching out to Manhattan.[82] Trump's father was initially skeptical about his son's ambitious ideas in the heart of New York City, but, as time went on, he came to accept them.

Trump used the techniques taught to him by his father in order to succeed. His biggest deal was revitalizing the Commodore Hotel into the Grand Hyatt, which is still known for its exceptional service.[83] In 1983, Trump made his

---

[82] "Donald Trump's Success Story." Investopedia. Last modified July 7, 2019.

[83] "Photos + Reviews." Grand Hyatt. http://www.hyatt.com/en-US/hotel/new-york/grand-hyatt-new-york/nycgh/photos-reviews.

mark in New York City by building the iconic Trump Tower located in midtown Manhattan. This 58-story building with its aesthetically pleasing architecture prospered from the economic boom of the 1980s.[84]

After reaping many benefits from the real estate market, Trump decided to build casinos. His first attempt was with the Taj Mahal Casino in Atlantic City, New Jersey. However, this proved to be an unsuccessful gamble. By 1989, the Trump Organization was in more debt than it could afford, and although its hotels and casino businesses filed for bankruptcy a number of times, the organization was able to recover from these adversities.[85] Despite these setbacks, Donald Trump did not give up. His acquisition of a 72-story building located in New York's financial district at 40 Wall Street would be one of Donald Trump's best real estate deals.

In 1982, brothers Joseph and Ralph Bernstein purchased 40 Wall Street, but it was unknown

---

[84] Ibid., "Donald Trump's Success Story"

[85] Ibid., "Donald Trump's Success Story"

how they had received their financing. It was discovered that the brothers were acting on behalf of Ferdinand Marcos, former president of the Philippines, who was deeply involved in the New York real estate market.[86] Countless evidences emerged that Marcos, along with his family and close associates, had robbed the Philippines economy of billions of dollars through embezzlements and other corrupt practices used to purchase New York real estate.[87] The brothers revealed this information in a court testimony, and after President Marcos fled the Philippines, ownership of 40 Wall Street was left in limbo, giving Donald Trump the perfect opportunity. With the building under no ownership, 40 Wall Street fell into chaos and decline. Many real estate companies made unsuccessful attempts to invest in the building but were unable to turn a

---

[86] Frantz, Douglas. "MARCOS N.Y. HOLDINGS $316 MILLION." Chicago Tribune. Last modified April 10, 1986.

[87] Encyclopaedia Britannica, Editors Of. "Ferdinand Marcos." Encyclopædia Britannica. Last modified September 24, 2019.

profit. In 1995, Trump invested more than $200 million in restorations, and 40 Wall Street became grander than ever before. Today, 40 Wall Street (The Trump Building) is one of the most successful commercial buildings in downtown Manhattan. Donald Trump's resilience and conviction were well-rewarded; the building and the area in which it resides have been thriving ever since.[88]

From that point on, Trump continued to excel in the real estate market, and his popularity increased further with the NBC reality TV show *The Apprentice.* According to some reports, Trump received $3 million per episode.[89] As Trump's fame and persona became well known, he decided it would be the perfect time for him to license his name and image. According to *Forbes,* Trump's real estate licensing business is among his most valuable assets, worth more than

---

[88] "A MANHATTAN SUCCESS STORY." 40 Wall Street.com. http://www.40wallstreet.com/our-story/.

[89] Ibid., "Donald Trump's Success Story"

$500 million.[90] Alongside his real estate properties, Trump affixed his name to many products, such as Trump Steaks, Trump Vodka, and *Trump Magazine.* Unfortunately, the majority of Trump's other products and businesses failed miserably, but he did not let those failures affect him.

There are two qualities a person needs to become successful: a strong work ethic and the ability to persevere through the failures and negative opinions of others. James K. Polk was criticized and betrayed by many politicians in the House of Representatives for his support of Andrew Jackson. While most would succumb to defeat, Polk fought back using his debate skills and knowledge. Likewise, many believed that Donald Trump would not become the successful businessman he is today. Although Trump experienced bankruptcies, he worked hard to overcome the challenges they brought. As a

---

[90] Olenski, Steve. "Donald Trump's Real Secret To Riches: Create A Brand And License It." Forbes. Last modified November 24, 2015.

result, Trump became prosperous and world-renowned. Both Polk and Trump experienced setbacks in which their resilience and perseverance were tested, but, like Trump himself once said, "What separates the winners from the losers is how a person reacts to each new twist of fate."[91]

---

[91] Ibid., "Donald Trump's Success Story."

Chapter 5: Spouses of Class

The first lady has an important function in the White House. She not only serves as the hostess for White House events, but she also plays an integral role in advocating for the political intentions of the president. Behind every successful president there is a great first lady. This statement is confirmed when discussing Sarah Childress Polk and Melania Trump.

Born and raised in a plantation near Murfreesboro, Tennessee, Sarah Childress was bestowed with many opportunities other women did not have. One of these was having formal schooling. Sarah attended the Moravian Female Academy in Salem, North Carolina, where she honed her skills in analyzing American politics.[92] This quality caught the eye of a young James K. Polk, and they married on New Year's Day 1824 at the home of the bride's parents. Sarah was 20 at the time, and James was 28.

Shortly after their marriage, Sarah and James

---

[92] "Sarah Polk." The White House Historical Association.

moved into a small cottage on the Polk family property in Columbia, Tennessee, where they lived until James's presidency. In an ordinary course of events, it was expected that Sarah would be busy with the demands of motherhood; however, it was soon evident that the Polk's would not be able to have any children because of James's surgery. As historian Amy S. Greenberg explains, "[Sarah Childress] was childless in an era where childbearing and rearing defined a woman's life."[93] As a result, she was able to devote more of her time to her husband's political work. Her father, a prominent land speculator, was deeply involved in politics, so it was not surprising that campaigning, gossiping, and coalition building came naturally to Sarah. When Polk served as a congressman in the House of Representatives, Sarah quickly emerged as his advocate, handling his correspondence. If her husband was giving a speech, Sarah would often be seen watching from the gallery.

---

[93] Greenberg, Amy S. "Lady First: The World of First Lady Sarah Polk." Speech, U.S. National Archives, Washington, DC, February 15, 2019.

Because Sarah Childress Polk was childless, she was able to throw herself into her husband's work. While most men would have been threatened by Sarah's strong opinions and political acumen, James embraced those qualities. On any given day, it was not surprising to see Sarah and James analyzing a political debate that had happened days prior. When Sarah arrived in Washington with her husband in the 1820s, she enjoyed its social scene and developed friendships with the wives of some of Washington's major politicians. She acquired a reputation as a lively conversationalist, which is what ultimately made her a successful political advocate for her husband.[94] Along with her social skills, Sarah Polk had a strict set of social standards. She refused to attend horse races or the theater, yet she was still able to maintain social political contacts of value to James.[95]

    Sarah and James formed a union of political

---

[94] Merry, *Vast Designs*, 32.

[95] Ibid., "Sarah Polk"

strength that was rare at the time. They were a harmonious and prosperous political team. Their bond was so strong that any time spent apart from each other was excruciating. Notably, many politicians in Washington sought the opinion of Sarah Childress Polk. Congressmen, senators, and justices of the Supreme Court depended on Sarah for inside information that would enable the successful navigation of the political scene in Washington.[96] While Sarah was in Washington, gossip was in the air. In the 1830s, John Eaton, Andrew Jackson's Secretary of War, was criticized by members of the Cabinet for marrying Peggy Eaton. Peggy Eaton was seen by Washington society as having no morals and thriving on the attention of male guests. After John married Peggy, rumors started to spread about her previous husband, John Timberlake. While Timberlake was off at sea, he died from pulmonary disease. People began to say that Peggy was to blame for the death because Timberlake was ashamed of her morals. Around

---

[96] Ibid., "Lady First: The World of First Lady Sarah Polk"

the time of Timberlake's death, Peggy and John met, and after a mourning period of one year, she married John on New Year's Day 1829.[97]

The responses from prominent political wives showed how much political power women had during this time. Many of them refused to speak to Peggy Eaton. Floride Calhoun, the wife of senator John C. Calhoun, led the wives of Jackson's Cabinet members to ostracize Peggy. Sarah Polk was caught right in the middle of the debate. Not surprisingly, Sarah sided with her husband and was not involved in the affair. She asserted to all Washington wives to put the needs of the country above dirty gossip.[98] This decision was a wise gamble for James, who managed to escape from this incident without having his reputation tarnished.

Sarah Childress was someone who advocated for her husband and wanted to see him succeed. She was skilled in social networking. Her

---

[97] "Peggy Eaton affair." American Historama.

[98] Ibid., "Lady First: The World of First Lady Sarah Polk."

interests in politics formed a union of political strength with her husband that would impact his executive actions as president. During Polk's campaign for the presidency, Sarah would use her political skills to influence party leaders as well as the regional press. One may argue that Sarah's political networking garnered support for her husband, ultimately making him president.

Although Melania Trump did not have the same political ambitions as Sarah Childress Polk, she is an influential first lady who shares similar political views with her husband. Melania was born in Novo Mesto, Slovenia, which was then part of communist Yugoslavia. At 18, Melania signed with a modeling agency in Milan where she worked until moving to New York in 1996. Melania met Donald Trump at a New York fashion party in 1998, and although she initially refused to date him, they became engaged in 2004. The following year, Donald and Melania were happily wed in a lavish Palm Beach, Florida ceremony. Melania later gave birth to her only child, Barron Trump, in 2006. After Barron was born, Melania left her modeling career, choosing instead to raise her child.[99]

Melania was forced into the national spotlight during the 2016 election. From the onset, many Americans believed that Melania Trump would not be an influential first lady. Controversies regarding her modeling career arose during the campaign when a newspaper erroneously reported that she had once worked as an escort. Melania sued the newspaper and received a settlement and apology.

Melania's credibility was further tarnished at the July Republican National Convention. Shortly after Melania gave her speech, the media attacked her, saying that sections of the speech had been plagiarized from the speech Michelle Obama had delivered during the 2008 Democratic National Convention.[100] During Trump's campaign, controversies surfaced regarding his indiscretions with other women. Despite these allegations, Melania Trump stood

---

[99] "Melania Trump." Biography.com. Last modified March 5, 2018.

[100] Ibid.

by her husband.[101]

When Melania first arrived at the White House in 2017, she made it her priority to make the executive mansion home for her family, and, like many other first ladies, she found a way to support a cause close to her heart: issues affecting children in the United States. In May 2018, she launched the BE BEST campaign, which focuses on some of the significant issues facing children today. This campaign has three objectives as it pertains to children: well-being, online safety, and opioid abuse. The first lady explained, "It remains our generation's moral imperative to take responsibility and help our children manage the many issues they are facing today . . ."[102]

When it came to the actions of the president, Melania went after her husband's attackers and praised his new policies when appropriate. This was evident after Trump signed into law

---

[101] Halper, Daniel. "Trump camp puts forward witness to refute sex assault claim" New York Post. Last modified October 14, 2016.

[102] "BE BEST First Lady Melania Trump's Initiative." White House. Gov.

legislation to curb the opioid epidemic, but public health advocates widely panned it. After the media started to attack the president, Melania responded with "I challenge the press to devote as much time to the lives lost—and the potential lives that could be saved—by dedicating the same amount of coverage that you do to idle gossip or trivial stories."[103]

Although Melania Trump and Sarah Childress Polk did not share the same involvement in the political affairs of their husbands, the first ladies wanted what was best for their men. Whereas Sarah was directly involved in the political ambitions of her husband, Melania has supported Trump in a less assuming role. However, both first ladies proved the point that behind every great president there is an influential, supportive first lady by his side.

---

[103] Itkowitz, Colby. "Melania Trump defends her husband by lecturing the media on their 'trivial stories.'" The Washington Post. Last modified March, 6, 2019.

Chapter 6: Rise to the Presidential Stage

As James K. Polk and Donald Trump became better known, their popularity with the American people also increased. None of them realized, however, that this popularity would lead them to the office of the presidency.

In the summer of 1838, Polk resigned as speaker of the House and returned to Tennessee to run for governor. The Tennessee Democrats begged Polk to run after Whig Governor Newton Cannon was elected. In the gubernatorial campaign, Polk brought his superior debating skills and strong political understanding of the issues of the day. He honed a campaign style that included ridicule and banter towards the Cannon administration. During debates, Polk would provide quick-witted arguments against both the proposed new national bank and increased infrastructure spending for items such as canals and roads. Often, Cannon was slow and methodical in planning his argument, and in some cases, he could not successfully deliver a rebuttal. This worked in James' favor, for he won the governor seat by a margin of 2,616 votes.[104] As governor, Polk would fulfill the core values of Jacksonian democracy, which gave the common man more access to the Democratic process.

Despite his popularity, Polk's first term as governor was not successful. Many states were still feeling the effects of the Panic of 1837, which had cost Martin Van Buren a chance of running for reelection in 1840. This economic environment made a successful governorship impossible. Polk's opportunities at reelection were also negatively impacted when Whig James C. Jones arrived on the political scene. Jones was nowhere near Polk when it came to debating the political events of the day, and he made up for this by acting like a fool and imposing ridicule upon the Polk administration. Despite Jones' rhetoric, Polk still ran a strong campaign, working tirelessly to connect with the people as best he could. However, he lost his reelection bid. In 1843, Polk ran once more with the same

---

[104] Merry, *Vast Designs*, 46.

outcome. The Jacksonian wave that had once dominated Tennessee was gone.[105] The once-successful James K. Polk had doubts that he could restore his political image. He returned to his home in Columbia, Tennessee, pondering his future in politics.

Following his defeat, Polk decided he would try his luck in the upcoming 1844 presidential election. As election season arrived, Polk had two goals: to capture the Democratic Party's vice-presidential nomination and to turn the now Whig-controlled Tennessee back to the Democrats.

When it came to the candidates, many people assumed the Democratic nomination would go to Martin Van Buren, who hoped to seek redemption after he had lost his chance for a second term in 1840. However, as a result of the Panic of 1837, there was a split in the Democratic Party. While many Democrats supported the previous economic policies of Van Buren, some saw that Van Buren's support of policies such as

---

[105] Ibid., 47.

the Specie Circular had lengthened the negative economic effects of the Panic of 1837. Van Buren supporters viewed these people as traitors of the Democratic Party and vowed to purge them from the party and elect Van Buren as president in 1844. Many Southern Democrats led by South Carolinian John C. Calhoun also opposed Van Buren for fear that a Northern president from a free state would support abolitionists and abandon the economic needs of the South.[106]

Despite the opposition, it was becoming highly likely that Van Buren would be the nominee. Polk believed his chances of becoming Van Buren's running mate depended on his ability to unite the Tennessee Democrats. In the now Whig-dominated state, Polk would have to run a vigorous campaign to muster support; fortunately, if there is one trait Polk possessed, it was hard work.

To be considered a Democratic candidate meant you had to closely interact with the common man. Unfortunately, Polk did not

---

[106] Ibid., 50-51.

display this social characteristic; however, he did not allow his social limitations to define his campaign. Even though he was not a people person, Polk mustered political support by interacting with the American people, giving stump speeches and telling jokes in a folksy manner.[107] By the time the Tennessee Democratic convention occurred on November 23, 1843, Polk had managed to reestablish his party leadership and persuade enough delegates to endorse him for the role of vice-president.[108]

Polk wrote a letter to Van Buren describing the events in Tennessee, hoping to be considered on the ticket with Van Buren as vice president. Van Buren responded to Polk's letter and referenced Andrew Jackson in his response when he said, "It is not to be endured that the Old Chief should go out of the world with his favorite Tennessee in Whig hands."[109] Based on this

---

[107] Ibid. "James K. Polk | PRESIDENTIAL podcast |"

[108] Merry, *Vast Designs,* 54.

[109] *Correspondence of James K. Polk,* 395.

response, Polk knew that despite the support from Tennessee delegates, he would have a difficult time becoming the vice-presidential candidate.

With defeat imminent, it appeared that Polk was being forgotten by the Democratic Party. His stance on the annexation of Texas, however, would help him regain his popularity. Texas annexation was an issue that previous presidents had avoided, for the annexation of Texas correlated directly with the issue of slavery. Under the Missouri Compromise of 1820, all newly admitted states below the north latitude line of 36° 30' would become slave states. Texas fell within this criterion. The issue of Texas annexation was rekindled when John Tyler became president.

John Tyler was the Whig vice-president of William Henry Harrison. After Harrison died 32 days after taking office, Tyler became president. Tyler can best be described as a "Whig In Name Only" (WINO). He was a states' rights Democrat who had only joined the Whig Party because he disliked the decision made by the Jackson administration regarding the Nullification Crisis. While he was in office, Tyler did not advance the Whig agenda, and the majority of his cabinet members resigned. This made him a president with no party affiliations.

On April 12, 1844, Tyler secretly negotiated a treaty of annexation with Texas. It provided that "Texas would become a U.S. territory eligible for admission later as one or more states. All Texan public lands would be ceded to the federal government, yet the boundaries between Mexico and Texas were not established."[110] Ten days later, the treaty went to the Senate. At the same time, a letter from Calhoun to Pakenham surfaced that explained why abolishing slavery in Texas would impact the "tranquility of the union." Pakenham, a British minister to the United States, had been lobbying for the abolition of slavery in America. On June 8, the Senate voted down Texas annexation by 35 to 16. For a treaty to pass the Senate, it needed a two-thirds majority. The

---

[110] Merk, Frederick. *Slavery and the Annexation of Texas.* New York: Alfred A. Knopf, 1972. 271-275. Howe, *What Hath God Wrought,* 679.

Texas annexation treaty was so unpopular that it did not even garner one-third of the Senate majority. Whigs from both the North and South opposed the treaty 27-1.[111] Tyler's first attempt at annexing Texas had not only gone wrong; it had now become an issue of focus in the upcoming presidential election.

Shortly before this failed attempt at Texas annexation, national nominating conventions were being held in which delegates were picking presidential candidates to run in 1844. On May 1, the Whigs had chosen their candidate in the form of former speaker of the House and senator from Kentucky, Henry Clay. The Whigs believed that the desire for more internal improvements as well as a stronger market economy would pave the way for America's third Whig president. Clay believed he would win the upcoming election, writing in a letter, "an irresistible current setting in towards me."[112]

---

[111] Freehling, William W. *Secessionists at Bay: 1776-1854*. New York, NY: Oxford Univ. Press, 1991. 431.

[112] Remini, Robert V. *Henry Clay: Statesman for the Union*. New York: W.W. Norton, 1991. 523.

The Democrats, on the other hand, could not decide on a candidate. While the Whig Party chose their candidate in one day, it took the Democrats three days—from May 27 to May 30—to select their candidate. Many Democrats believed Martin Van Buren would be their nominee, but while Van Buren controlled a simple majority of the delegates, he failed to muster the two-thirds majority needed.[113] As the balloting continued, Van Buren continuously lost support and subsequently the nomination because he publicly opposed Texas annexation. This action angered many Southern Democrats, costing Van Buren their votes.

Despite many upsets in his campaign to become vice-president, Polk was still involved in the election and vying for the nomination. While he believed in the same principles as Van Buren, such as having an Independent Treasury, he took a firm stance on the Texas issue. As a strict expansionist, Polk believed Texas needed to

---

[113] Howe, Daniel Walker. What Hath God Wrought: The Transformation of America, 1815-1848. New York: Oxford University Press, 2007. 682.

become part of the United States, even if it meant the country would go to war with Mexico. This doctrine of imperialism was popular with many Southern Democrats, resulting in Polk winning the ninth presidential ballot and thus becoming the Democratic nominee for president. After the nomination, the Democrats established their party platform:

"Resolved, That our title to the whole of the Territory of Oregon is clear and unquestionable; that no portion of the same ought to be ceded to England or any other power, and that the re-occupation of Oregon and the re-annexation of Texas at the earliest practicable period are great American measures, which this Convention recommends to the cordial support of the Democracy of the Union."[114]

No one expected that Polk would run for president; after all, he was not a national figure like Andrew Jackson was. So why was he

---

[114] Porter, Kirk H., and Donald Bruce Johnson. *National Party Platforms, 1840-1968*. Urbana: University of Illinois Press, 1970.

selected? The answer is simple: Polk appealed to the American people's strong emotions of patriotism and nationalism. This same strategy would be used years later when Donald Trump would be nominated by the Republican Party to run for president.

While Trump did not possess the same political acumen as James K. Polk, becoming president was the topic of many TV interviews. An issue that Trump discussed constantly was foreign policy. Over the course of his lifetime, Trump had despised politicians because, when it came to trade with other foreign nations, America was weak. He could not stand the fact that Washington allowed other countries to dictate American policies regarding trade. In a 1988 appearance on The Oprah Winfrey Show, Trump criticized foreign policy, saying the United States does not fight against unfair trade. When Trump was later asked whether he would ever run for the executive office, he explained, "I just don't think I have the inclination to do it. I love what I am doing right now, but I do get tired of seeing what is going on with this country. . . making other countries live like kings while we do not."[115] Like the Jacksonian Democrats of the 1840s, Trump believed, "On every major issue affecting this country, the people are right and the governing elite are wrong."[116] When Trump saw how the government elitists were not acting in the best interests of the common electorate, he decided to run for office.

Regarding his party affiliations, Trump was a Republican, and his stance on issues affecting America showed it. In 1999, Trump switched his voter registration from the Republican Party to the Reform Party, whose main goal was to put power back into the hands of everyday citizens and make government accessible to everyone.[117]

---

[115] *The Oprah Winfrey Show*. "Donald Trump Teases a President Bid During a 1988 Oprah Show." Hosted by Oprah Winfrey. Aired 1988, on OWN.

[116] Cohen, Kelly. "Trump: America needs 'bold infusion of popular will.'" Washington Examiner. Last modified April 15, 2016.

[117] Smith, Nicole. "Overview of the Reform Party in America." Article Myriad. Last modified December 7, 2011.

He ran a campaign to become the nominee for the Reform Party in the 2000 election, focusing his campaign on issues of fair trade and eliminating the national debt. While on the campaign trail, Trump displayed a sense of confidence. In an airing of Jay Leno, Trump professed, "I feel in my gut, in my heart that I can win. If I do win, I would save people a lot of green."[118] Despite his confidence, Trump publicly ended his campaign on an airing of the Today Show on February 14, 2000.

After his unsuccessful presidential campaign, Trump rejoined the Republican Party and maintained a high public profile during the 2012 presidential election, endorsing Mitt Romney for president.

On June 16, 2015, Donald Trump announced to the American public from Trump Tower that he would be running for president in 2016. In his campaign speech, Trump criticized politicians, saying they were the ones destroying the United States both politically and economically. He promised to create new job opportunities and

---

[118] *Donald Trump on Jay Leno*. NBC, December 7, 1999.

reduce the influence of special interest groups in Washington, D.C. When it came to foreign policy, Trump pledged to impose tariffs on countries that engaged in trade policies that were unfair to the United States. Perhaps his most desirable promise was a border wall along the U.S.-Mexico border to prevent illegal immigration. This last promise appealed to working-class Americans who were losing their jobs while the government was giving benefits to illegal immigrants.[119]

These were issues that the electorate wanted to see fixed. Donald Trump was the candidate who would Make America Great Again. On July 21, 2016, Trump was selected to become the Republican nominee for president of the United States. Trump faced off against well-seasoned Democratic politician Hillary Clinton for the presidency. In the coming months, the nation would have to make a decision during the most

---

[119] Trump, Donald J. "Donald Trump Announces His 2016 Presidential Bid." Trump Tower, June 16 2015, New York City. Address.

heated presidential campaign modern America had ever seen.

As Donald Trump and James K. Polk entered their respective presidential races, the American people started to formulate their own opinions. Both of the candidates would experience backlash from Washington politicians and elitists; however, if there was one political force that both men had, it was the emotional appeal to the middle and working-class ideals of nationalism and patriotism.

Chapter 7: The Common Man's Campaign

In a presidential election, a candidate's campaign strategy plays an essential role in the election outcome. In the respective cases of Polk and Trump, a successful campaign included elements of patriotism and a connection between the candidate and the voter.

After Polk was chosen to be the Democratic nominee for president, he received a letter from the convention committee requesting his acceptance of the nomination. Responding on June 12, he wrote:

"It has been well observed that the office of President of the United States should neither be sought nor declined. I have never sought it, nor should I feel at liberty to decline it, if conferred upon me by the voluntary suffrages of my Fellow Citizens."[120]

---

[120] Polk, James K. Letter to Democratic National Convention, "James K. Polk to the Committee of the Democratic National Convention accepting the Democratic presidential nomination," June 12, 1844. Library of Congress, Washington, DC.

Three months later, the executive committee of the Democratic Association in Washington, D.C., proclaimed:

"A National Bank, Distribution, and Triple Taxation are the evils we apprehend from the election of Henry Clay, a free government, and taxation for public purposes only, we expect from the election of James K. Polk."[121]

Meanwhile, the Whig candidate, Henry Clay, was running a strong campaign in his home state of Kentucky. Clay was viewed as a national hero by the Whigs. Ballads such as "A Song for the Man" praised Clay for his political actions, such as The American System, which aimed to connect America through a system of internal improvements, resulting in a unified market economy. He was also praised for legislation such as the Compromise Tariff of 1833, which

---

[121] Executive committee of the Democratic association. "Circular from the Executive committee of the Democratic association of Washington City.," September 1844. Library of Congress,

lowered tariff rates by 8 percent over 10 years. The passage of this pivotal piece of legislation ended the Nullification Crisis in South Carolina, caused by a high tariff in 1832.[122] One particular ballad portrays Henry Clay as the "Whig Chief" who would make the Whig Party prosperous. The Whigs sang this triumphant ballad, proclaiming:

"In the chair of state, due none but the great, the world shall our chieftain see; for triumph we must, our cause is just, and perfect our Union be! For victor comes, mid the roll of drums, with his glorious Whig array."[123]

Whig ballads, banners, and political cartoons circulated across the United States during the election period. As election day approached, it seemed Henry Clay would finally win the

---

[122] Russell, Henry. "A song for the man, a Henry Clay ballad." 1844. Library of Congress, Washington, DC.

[123] Warland, J. H., and E. H. Wade. "The Whig Chief." 1844. Library of Congress, Washington, DC.

presidency, becoming America's third Whig president. However, the Polk campaign had other plans.

When it came to campaigning, the Democrats did not have the patriotic ballads of the Whig Party. There was one song written about Polk, titled "Jimmy Polk of Tennessee." This song was written by the Whigs to mock the Democrats for choosing Polk as a candidate. The chorus sung:

"But hark, the people rising say that is not the man

to cope with Clay. Ha, ha, such a nominee, Jimmy

Polk of Tennessee!"[124]

However, other methods of campaigning against Clay were effective. Polk supporters used various political cartoons aimed to damage Clay's popularity. A popular pro-Polk cartoon titled "Texas Coming In" praised Polk's campaign promise that called for the annexation

---

[124] *Jimmy Polk of Tennessee.* Composed by J. Greiner, 1844.

of Texas. In the cartoon, Polk is standing on the right side of a bridge spanning "salt river,"[125]* holding an American flag, and welcoming a steamboat-like vessel named Texas into the United States. Stephen Austin, the "Father of Texas," shouts, "All hail to James K. Polk, the friend of our country!" Meanwhile, Whigs such as Henry Clay are being dragged into the "salt river." As Clay holds onto the rope, which is pulling him into the river, he shouts, "Curse the day that I ever got hold of this rope! This is a bad place to let go of it—but I must!"[126]

After this attack, the Whigs fought back by publishing political cartoons in the same way Polk supporters had done. Shortly after the "Texas Coming In" cartoon was published, Whig supporters created a cartoon titled "Bursting the Balloon." In the bottom left, Clay supporters can be seen shouting, "Hurrah! Hurrah, for the

---

[125] *"Salt River" was a colloquialism for political misfortune or failure during this period.

[126] Baillie, James S., and H. Bucholzer. *Texas Coming in.* June 28, 1844. Illustration. Library of Congress, Washington, DC.

people's choice [Clay], mounts upward like an eagle." As Henry Clay and his vice-presidential nominee Theodore Frelinghuysen rise triumphantly in a balloon to the presidential chair in the heavens, Clay punctures the ascending balloon of the Democrats led by Polk with an American flag. As Polk plunges into the water, Clay yells, "Good-bye, Polk, you'll find it much easier traveling in that direction!"[127] This pro-Whig cartoon portrayed the Democrats as a party that was heading towards failure, all because they had selected James K. Polk to be their presidential candidate.

The Whigs published more political cartoons, ballads, banners, and other political paraphernalia supporting their candidate Henry Clay and denouncing Polk. The Whigs were confident Clay would be elected president and would lead the American republic into prosperity, yet they did not keep a close eye on the issues of westward expansion. On the

---

[127] Baillie, James S., and H. Bucholzer. *Bursting the Balloon*. 1844. Illustration. Library of Congress, Washington, DC.

campaign trail, Clay promoted higher tariffs, more internal improvements, and a re-established national bank to replace the one that had been eliminated by the Jackson administration. What the Whigs did not realize was that America was changing, and while some of them viewed Clay's points as valid, the electorate was focusing on other issues.

James K. Polk's campaign was one of nationalism and expansionism. Polk was a firm believer in the doctrine of Manifest Destiny. The term "Manifest Destiny" was coined by John L. O'Sullivan, an American columnist and editor during the 1840s. O'Sullivan believed it was America's God-given right to expand from sea to shining sea. Polk used this doctrine to propose the annexation of Texas and the acquisition of the entire Oregon Territory from Britain. His supporters coined the phrase "Fifty-four Forty or Fight!" conveying the intention to either claim the whole Oregon Territory for the United States or go to war with the British. Even though Polk was an expansionist who wanted to acquire the Oregon Territory, he did not want a war with the powerful British Empire because he knew that the American army and navy was not equipped to win against it. Polk's campaign of patriotism and nationalism resonated with the common man and turned the tide of the election in his favor.

Trump's presidential campaign strategy was also rooted in the American ideals of patriotism and nationalism. His doctrine of improving the lives of the average American and putting America first when it came to policy decisions made him a popular candidate. His campaign message was refreshing because he wanted the average citizen to benefit from his policies. This was unheard of in Washington, where lobbyists and special interest groups ruled. Throughout the election, Democrats denounced Trump, saying he was a womanizer, a racist, and unfit to be a leader. Instead of backing down, Trump fought back against these negative comments.

During his run for president, Trump held rallies regularly. When news of a Trump rally was announced, venues were filled, and a reinvigorated spirit of American nationalism flourished. As Trump walked on stage to give his monologue to the American people, one might hear Lee Greenwood's "God Bless the USA" playing as the crowd erupts in applause for their future president. When Trump arrived at the podium, he was jovial and cracked jokes with the audience. One of the characteristics that his audience admired about Trump was the absence of a politician's filter; he said what was on his mind, and while this angered the media and the Washington elite, Trump supporters were enthusiastic. At every campaign rally, Trump attacked the press for being dishonest towards the American people. Trump especially attacked CNN, which he called the Clinton News Network, saying to one reporter, "You're with CNN? You people do not cover us accurately at all!"[128] It seemed that every Trump rally was not complete without an attack on the "Fake News" media.

Trump also used his rallies to attack politicians who attacked his supporters. When Hillary

---

[128] "Donald Trump's Funniest Insults and Comebacks." *YouTube*. Posted by Mark Dice, December 22, 2016.

Clinton said, "You could put half of Trump supporters into what I call a basket of deplorables,"[129] Trump responded with, "My opponent slanders you as deplorable and irredeemable; I call you hard-working American patriots who love your country and want a better future for all of our people."[130] Along the campaign trail, Trump advocated for the American people to be treated fairly by the government, saying at one rally, "There's a silent majority out there who is tired of being pushed around, kicked around, and being led by stupid people!"[131] Trump's campaign slogan, "Make America Great Again," rallied even more supporters who wanted to return to a period in

---

[129] Thomas, Cal. "'The 'Deplorables': Hillary reveals her contempt for everyday Americans." The Washington Times. Last modified September 12, 2016

[130] Schwartz, Ian. "Trump: While Hillary Slanders You As Deplorable, I Call You Hard-Working American Patriots." Real Clear Politics. Last modified September 13, 2016.

[131] "Donald Trump: candidate's most controversial campaign moments." Video. *YouTube*. Posted by Channel 4 News, July 21, 2015.

which the American economy was once again the envy of the world.

With their goals set and their support mustered, both James K. Polk and Donald J. Trump would be ready to run strong campaigns that echoed the values of patriotism, nationalism, and support for the common man. As the candidates ran their respective campaigns, others tried to discredit them at every turn. This group of people consisted of newspaper reporters and the mainstream media, who stopped at nothing to portray these candidates in a negative light.

Chapter 8: The Biased Press

Throughout history, the media has been an integral part of the American political system. It provides the public with access to news and editorial opinions on various political positions and policies. In presidential elections, the media holds a vital role in delivering information on party policies and platforms. When it comes to portraying presidential candidates, however, individual media outlets usually show bias towards one candidate. This was certainly true for the media reports during the Polk and Trump campaigns.

During the 1844 election, newspapers largely served as the source of information in a candidate's campaign. Newspapers had a large amount of influence on the American people; as historian Daniel Walker Howe mentions, "Many if not most newspapers of the [19th century] were organs of a political party or faction within a party, existing not to make a profit but to propagate a point of view."[132] Because of the many congressional speeches and "circular letters" published in local newspapers, it was easy for each political party to portray different interpretations and spin the narrative.

Shortly after the Democratic National Convention in Baltimore, Whig newspapers such as the *New York Daily Tribune* attacked Polk, the recently nominated "dark horse" candidate. In the June 1 issue, the following was written:

"... James K. Polk, certainly not more than a third rate politician—who never devised a measure nor said a thing worth remembering—a tolerable stump speaker, with a liberal flow of words, but rather too much of a buffoon–who became Governor of Tennessee in 1839 because the Whigs ran a candidate who could not speak and would not drink–but was beaten on the stump, and turned out in a fair face-to-face contest in 1841, by James C. Jones, then a young man untried and unknown, and beaten again by a larger majority in '43–is to be the candidate for a once

---

[132] Howe, *What Hath God Wrought*, 228.

powerful party for President! Indeed, the man beaten twice in succession by a stripling of his state, would hardly seem the man to pit against Henry Clay."[133]

Whig newspapers also attacked Polk's plan and the executive actions he would take if he became president. One such attack was on Polk's view of tariffs. After the passage of the Tariff of 1842, the terms under the Compromise Tariff of 1833 were no longer in effect. This led to tariff rates on some goods to increase by nearly 32 percent. Because of this high tariff rate, there was a sharp decline in foreign trade; however, the prices of Northern manufactured products also increased substantially. Polk's response to the tariff was conveyed in a pamphlet acquired by the *Alexandria Gazette* from editors of the *Memphis Eagle*. Polk's view on the tariff was as follows: "All who have observed my course, know that I have at all times been opposed to the protective tariff policy. I am in favor of a tariff for revenue,

---

[133] Greeley, Horace, and Thomas McElrath. "The Extraordinary Doings at Baltimore-What They Mean." *New-York Daily Tribune*, June 1, 1844.

and opposed to a tariff for protection." Edgar Snowden, the publisher of the *Alexandria Gazette*, later commented, "It is thus that [Polk] avows himself the enemy of American labor."[134] Polk's view on tariff policy did not appeal to voters in the North, where American manufacturing was flourishing and selling expensive goods to the Southern states.

Another issue that surfaced during the presidential campaign was the issue of slavery. Throughout his political career, Polk felt the preservation of the union should be a national objective, and therefore, he kept silent on the issue.[135] He knew that this issue would ultimately require resolution, but he preferred to defer the matter to future presidents after he achieved his Manifest Destiny objectives.

In addition to the media scrutiny on Polk's policies, the fiber of his moral character was questioned. During the election, Whig

---

[134] *Alexandria Gazette*, September 2, 1844.

[135] Marsh, Richard Dean. "James K. Polk and Slavery." Master's thesis, University of North Texas, 1977.

newspapers questioned Polk's religious beliefs, character, and support of American interests. In an issue of *The New York Daily Tribune*, it was written:

"As to James K. Polk, the manner in which he is commended to personal favor excites in us daily a deeper dislike to him. The silly trick of christening him 'Young Hickory' and then pretending that the Whigs had given him that name; the lying assertion that he was a church member and a Temperance man; the dirty trick of inquiring through the Journal of Commerce whether he were not a Catholic, and avowing that would be a ground of refusing to vote for him–(to excite the Catholics in his favor, and then win Protestants also by contradicting the story) . . ."[136]

The *Richmond Palladium* described the Democratic nominee as:

". . . a man who has always voted against and acted

---

[136] Greeley, Horace. "James K. Polk." *New-York Daily Tribune*, August 16, 1844.

THE BIASED PRESS

against [the interests of the American people] and who, should he be elected, will, judging from his votes and acts while in Congress, never recommended one measure for your benefit. . ."[137]

The *Carroll Free Press* even provided a long list of Polk's wrongdoings, which included:

"[Voting] against bills for the relief of the surviving officers and soldiers of the [American] Revolution . . ., [being] presented as a nuisance by a Grand Jury of his own State, and [voting] against renumerating the patriot [former President James Monroe], for property that he had sacrificed in defense of his country. . ."[138]

Elaborating on the final point made by the

---

[137] Holloway, D. P., and B.W. Davis. "Second Session 23d Congress." *Richmond Palladium* (Richmond, VA), August 9, 1844.

[138] Brown, Van, and T. W. Collier. "Keep It Before The People." *Carroll Free Press* (Carrollton, OH), August 9, 1844.

Carroll Free Press, James Monroe was regularly referred to as a patriot by many during this time because he had served as a lieutenant under George Washington during the American Revolution. After serving two terms as president, Monroe's personal finances ran out of control, and he was $75,000 in debt.[139] Monroe continuedly went to Congress and asked if he could be reimbursed because of his contributions as president and to American independence from Great Britain. Although Congress gave Monroe what he asked for, Polk, then a congressman from Tennessee, voted against the reimbursement.

Despite the countless attacks made on Polk, there were newspapers that agreed with his expansionist policies and wanted to see him ascend to the presidency. One such example was seen in the Ohio *Cadiz Sentinel*, where a letter praising Polk for his accomplishments and attributes was presented. It described Polk's tenure as a member of the House of

---

[139] The Independent, Editors Of. "James Monroe." The Independent. Last modified January 17, 2009.

THE BIASED PRESS

Representatives and speaker of the House, and it concludes with:

> "Ultimately, [Polk's political acumen] and correct reasoning will convince the impartial and intelligent of all parties that he is a man of talents and a statesman; and well qualified to discharge all the duties of the office of President of the United States, with honor to himself and his country."[140]

Numerous newspapers presented Polk in various ways. While some viciously attacked him, others painted him positively.

As technology improved, the media machine increased its influence on the American people. The invention of television, the smartphone, and radio along with the development of social media outlets such as YouTube, Instagram, Facebook, and Twitter allowed news to be dispersed rapidly. Now, information on candidates is available immediately. In Polk's time, it would take days for people to hear about recent political

---

[140] Harper, Lecky. "Interesting Correspondence" *The Cadiz Sentinel* (OH), September 11, 1844.

developments in Washington. Now, Americans can receive political news in a fraction of a second. This improvement in delivery time has provided the media with better tools to convey different political views.

After Trump announced that he was running for president in 2016, the mainstream media that supported the views of the Democratic Party—composed of ABC, CBS, CNN, NBC, and MSNBC—immediately began a negative campaign against him. During the 2016 campaign season, it was shocking if Donald Trump did not make the news. For months, the left-wing media reported nothing else but negative comments on Trump. While the main intentions of the left-wing media were to make Trump an unfavorable candidate by attacking his lack of political experience and temperament, this strategy backfired as he became more popular among the electorate. Although Trump was not a politician and lacked political experience, he routinely said, even long before the 2016 election, that he would be a better politician than the ones currently in Washington.

In an NBC interview from the 1980s, Trump remarked, "I think I am pretty outspoken and that's probably not a good thing in the terms of a politician. But, if someone got elected with this trait, they could really get things done."[141]

Throughout his campaign, Trump gained a reputation of being arrogant and ignorant by the left-leaning wing of the media. Many political analysts from these media outlets commented on Trump's lack of political experience, saying he did not deserve to run in the election. The media may have seen Donald Trump as incompetent, but the American people saw him as someone who was capable of accomplishing his pro-America agenda.

Another tactic used by the left-wing media was interviewing influential Americans, such as celebrities, in the hope that they would provide negative comments on Trump. Many celebrities voiced their negative opinions on the presidential candidate and gave the mainstream media what

---

[141] "1980s: How Donald Trump Created Donald Trump | NBC News." Video. YouTube. Posted by NBC News, July 6, 2016.

they wanted. One celebrity who strongly expressed her views on the Republican nominee was Cher, an influential female pop singer. She said to one interviewer, "Someone who would bring down the country because he doesn't win, does not deserve anything. Trump deserves nothing. He does not deserve any kind of respect or loyalty; I don't think he has two moral fibers to rub together. He wants to be the king, but he doesn't want to do the work."[142] Not only did this comment attack Trump's morality, but it also attacked his work ethic. Other disparaging remarks were made by celebrities like Tom Hanks, who said in one interview, "I think [Trump] will be president of the United States right about the time that spaceships come down filled with dinosaurs in red capes!"[143] Perhaps one of the worst forms of bias against the Republican candidate was seen at the 2016 White

---

[142] "Cher on Trump: 'I'd put my fist through his face.'" Video. *YouTube*. Posted by Associated Press, October 20, 2016.

[143] Alter, Charlotte. "Tom Hanks Says Donald Trump Will Be President When 'Spaceships Come Down.'" *Time*

House Correspondents' Dinner. Every year, celebrities, politicians, and media of both the left and right points of view travel to Washington, D.C., and listen to jokes about politicians. In Obama's last White House Correspondents' Dinner as president, he comically remarked:

"I am a little hurt that [Trump] is not here tonight. You got a room full of reporters, celebrities, cameras, and he says no. Is this dinner tacky for the Donald? What could he possibly be doing instead? Is he at home eating a Trump Steak? Tweeting out insults to Angela Merkel? The Republican establishment is shocked that Trump is their most likely nominee; they say Donald lacks the foreign policy experience. I have a lot more material, but I am going to show some restraint. I think we can all agree from the start he's gotten the appropriate amount of coverage befitting the seriousness of his candidacy!"[144]

---

[144] "Obama White House Correspondents Dinner 2016 | President Obama's FULL SPEECH" Video. YouTube. Posted by ABC News, May 1, 2016.

As Obama cracked his jokes, many of the attendees laughed, for they, at the time, firmly believed that because of Trump's demeanor, he would never be elected president.

Despite the negativity from Democratic media outlets, Republican media outlets supported Trump. Outlets such as Fox News portrayed Trump positively, and they attacked Democratic media outlets for their accusations. Sean Hannity, a Fox News reporter, even said:

> "The media already had its chance to cover Donald Trump fairly and honestly; they blew it! And in my opinion, it's time to reevaluate the press in this country . . . they should not have the privilege of covering Trump on behalf of the American people."[145]

As the media reported their opinions on the Republican candidate, Trump continued to run his campaign to "Make America Great Again." In his well-attended rallies, Trump continued to

---

[145] "Hannity: So-called unbiased media had to eat their words." Video. YouTube. Posted by Fox News, November 23, 2016.

label the left-wing media as dishonest. Trump supporters were also tired of the media coverage. The daily dose of the left-wing media making fun of the Republican nominee served as comic relief for Republicans, and it ultimately allowed Trump supporters to coin the phrase "Trump Derangement Syndrome."

Even though the media of today has dramatically expanded since it first appeared in the form of newspapers in the 1800s, it still serves the same purpose: to influence the American people into believing every story it portrays. The media also slanders any influential person who does not align with their political views. Both Polk and Trump felt the full effects of these tactics, yet they managed to emerge from these attacks as strong presidential candidates. The American people now had to decide what information they would believe as election day approached.

Chapter 9: The Day of Utmost Importance

After months of campaigning, election day arrived, and the American people had an important decision to make both in 1844 and 2016. Do they vote for the well-seasoned politician, or do they vote for the underdog who is less experienced in the political arena but whose platform is rooted in American nationalism and patriotism?

American public opinion was definitely divided during the election of 1844, for the candidates each had drastically different goals for the country.[146] The Whigs believed Henry Clay would finally become their president. He was the most well-known politician of his time, and his agenda had a broad appeal to the electorate in both the North and the South. However, the issue of Texas annexation would prove to be his demise.

When it came to the Texas issue, Henry Clay

---

[146] Howe, *What Hath God Wrought*, 686.

was known to change points regularly. On April 17, 1844, Clay warned in the Raleigh Letter that Texas annexation would spark a war with Mexico and allow slavery to spread as a result of the Missouri compromise of 1820.[147] Another factor that greatly impacted the Whigs during this election was their policy agenda. Since he began running for president, Clay had vowed to uphold the American System, which was a three-part plan to develop a unified national economy. He also vowed to continue social reforms, including the expansion of women's rights and the temperance movement.[148] However, these were not the issues Americans were concerned about during this period. The controversial issue at the forefront of almost every presidential election at the time was the continued legality of slavery. Northern Whigs were opposed to the continuation of slavery, while Southern

---

[147] Clay, Henry, Melba Porter Hay, and Carol Reardon. *The Papers of Henry Clay: Candidate, Compromiser, Elder Statesman, Jan. 1, 1844-June 29, 1852*. Lexington, Ky.: University Press of Kentucky, 1991.41-46.

[148] Ibid.

Democrats supported the institution for economic reasons. To appeal to the South, Clay wrote in his Alabama letter that he would be glad to see Texas annexed, but it was just not the right time. Clay's noncommittal position negatively impacted his credibility with voters.

Polk realized that to appeal to both Northern and Southern Democrats and achieve his Manifest Destiny doctrine, he needed to propose a compromise. During the campaign, he appealed to Southerners by proposing the annexation of Texas as a slave state, and he also appealed to Northerners by proposing the annexation of the Oregon Territory from Britain as a free state. Through this compromise, the sectional balance and union would be preserved. Polk knew his Manifest Destiny objectives would not be achieved without delaying and deferring on this issue.

The election was extremely close. Polk gained the majority of his support in the southwest, where his manifest destiny doctrine gained popularity. Surprisingly, he won the Northern states of New York and Pennsylvania, which added 62 electoral votes to his total. Even though Clay won the remaining states in the North, he lost New York and Pennsylvania, which were states he needed to win.[149] In the end, Polk received 170 electoral votes to Clay's 105. Additionally, even though Polk won the majority of the electoral vote, the popular vote was extremely close. Polk gained 49.5% of the popular vote, Clay 48.1%, and the other 2% went to James Birney of the Liberty Party, which gained support after Clay had changed his position on Texas.[150] James K. Polk was elected the eleventh president of the United States and became one of the first "dark horse" candidates in American history.

The 2016 election had a similar result. Trump campaigned on a platform to restore America's greatness, which was popular with the average American but not with the coastal elitists. During

---

[149] Holt, Michael F. *The Rise and Fall of the American Whig Party: Jacksonian Politics and the Onset of the Civil War*. New York: Oxford University Press, 1999. 199-201.

[150] Howe, *What Hath God Wrought*, 686.

the campaign, the left-wing media continued to disparage Trump. Even Hillary Clinton said in an MSNBC interview, "I do not think that Donald Trump will be the president-elect, and if I am the nominee, it certainly will not happen."[151] This was the prevailing notion preached by the left-wing mainstream media. Many experts predicted the outcomes on electoral maps, showing a landslide victory for Clinton. Some experts predicted that Republican states such as South Carolina and Texas would vote Democrat in 2016. When election day came on November 8, the predictions that had been made by the pro-Clinton media were proven wrong.

Americans had mixed feelings coming into election day 2016. As polling places closed, the mainstream media began broadcasting polling results. Trump was gaining the majority of electoral votes from the South and Midwest, while Clinton was gaining the majority of electoral votes in the Northeast and on the West

---

[151] "Hillary Clinton On Possibility of President Donald Trump | Rachel Maddow| MSNBC." Video. *YouTube*. Posted by MSNBC, March 11, 2016.

THE DAY OF UTMOST IMPORTANCE

coast. Since the candidates were gaining electoral votes in their respective strongholds, it came down to the swing states. Two of the first swing states to be declared for Trump were Ohio, with 52% of the vote, and Florida, with 49% of the vote. Finally, one of the most crucial swing states, Pennsylvania, went to Trump.[152] The polls in these states had initially projected significant Clinton wins; however, the promise to "Make America Great Again" had proven appeal to the majority of the electorate.

In the early morning of November 9, Hillary Clinton called Donald Trump and conceded the election. Trump would become the forty-fifth president of the United States. He had lost the popular vote by a margin of 48.2% to 46.1% due to California voting overwhelmingly for Clinton by a margin of 4.3 million voters. Trump had earned 304 electoral votes to Clinton's 227.[153]

---

[152] "Election Night 2016 - Highlights." Video. *YouTube*. Posted by NBC News, November 26, 2016.

[153] "2016 Election Results." 270towin. http://www.270towin.com/historical-presidential-elections/timeline/.

With victory secured, Trump proclaimed in his victory speech, "I pledge to every citizen of our land that I will be president for all Americans, and this is so important to me."[154] Another political underdog had become president.

The elections of 1844 and 2016 were similar because in both, the underdog, not the experienced politician, had prevailed. Both James K. Polk and Donald J. Trump became presidents because they appealed to the American ideals of nationalism and patriotism. They became presidents because of their vision for a stronger America.

---

[154] "Waves of Emotions After a Trump Victory." Video. YouTube. Posted by ABC News, November 10, 2016.

Part 2: The Influential Presidency

Chapter 10: Americans in Disarray

James K. Polk and Donald J. Trump won their respective elections. The popular vote, however, showed how divided the American public was with the result (Polk had garnered 49.5% of the vote, and Trump 46.1%).

The 1844 election proved to be disastrous for the Whigs. They were hoping 1844 would be the year when their plan for unity through centralized power would come to fruition. Unfortunately, the American people did not side with this view on election day and voted for an expansionist who dreamed of making America a powerful empire. As a way to air out their grievances, the Whigs relied on newspapers to publish their opinions. The *National Intelligencer* made this bold claim:

> "The larger portion of the educated and informed people of the land voted for Clay, while the larger portion of those neither educated nor well-informed voted for their successful opponents."[155]

---

[155] Smith, Samuel Harrison. *The National Intelligencer*. November, 1844.

This statement confirmed the arrogance of Whig Party supporters. It was becoming apparent that the Whigs were not a party for the common people.

Even though Polk was chosen by the American public to be president, the Whigs questioned the results of the election. Polk had won a majority of the electoral votes, but the popular vote had been extremely close. *The Whig Standard* commented:

> "Henry Clay has received in this election more [popular] votes than were ever given before to any man for any office in this country, a fact which demonstrates that the Whig party is now of itself stronger than at any time since its formation . . . Mr. Clay's plurality over Polk in Massachusetts is greater than the majority of the states of New York, Pennsylvania, and Virginia, combined."[156]

This was the mantra of many Whig

---

[156] Towers, John T. "Henry Clay and the Whig Party." *The Whig Standard* (Washington, DC), November 15, 1844.

newspapers regarding the election of 1844. Although Clay had gained the majority of the popular vote in most Northern states, Polk's plurality in New York and Pennsylvania angered many Whigs because these were states that they believed should have gone for Clay.

A concern for Whigs after the election was that they anticipated a decline in Northern manufacturing as well as an increase in unemployment. Industries in the North, such as textile mills, relied on protectionist tariffs, which made
European goods more expensive and thus made American products more competitive. With the election of Polk, Northern industrialists became increasingly worried. The *New York Daily Tribune* explained:

> "If the results of this election should prove still more disastrous–as we do not see how they can fail to do–if the overthrow of the protective tariff should transfer the making of our wares and fabrics from our workingmen to those of Europe . . . half of the workingmen in our factories and workshops will be

unemployed. *Let those who have battled faithfully and zealously to avert these calamities be their last victims.* [The Democrats] have not regarded with envy or hatred the prosperity of their employers . . . the people who afford them sustenance and shelter."[157]

Despite what many Whig Party members said, Polk's presidency did not result in an increase in unemployment in America. Instead, his economic policy contributed to a prosperous country. After the election, Whigs believed "the country will go to ruin because Mr. Polk was elected President."[158] Because Polk was an expansionist and wanted to annex Texas, Northern Whigs feared for war with Mexico and the expansion of slavery under the Missouri Compromise of 1820.

It is important to note that although the abolitionists were a wing of the Whig Party, they

---

[157] "The Results of the Results." *The New York Daily Tribune,* November 12, 1844.

[158] Jones, J.B. "Ruin." *The Daily Madisonian* (Washington, DC), November 16, 1844.

were more adamant about ending the institution of slavery. Remember, Clay lost the abolitionist vote in states such as New York because he had supported the postponement of the annexation of Texas instead of its prevention.

Although the election of James K. Polk was met with divisiveness, the lives of most Americans went on as usual and even improved. Such attacks on winners of an election continue to be commonplace, as was evidenced by the election of Donald J. Trump 172 years later.

Americans were sharply divided after the election of Donald Trump, as he had received 46.1% of the popular vote. Republican supporters were eager for Inauguration Day to occur so that President-elect Trump could begin revitalizing the American nation. On the other hand, the Democrats had responded with fear and anger. During election night, the mood among the Democrats was somber. Every state the Democrats had thought would go to Clinton went to Trump.

The left-wing media that had attacked Trump since the start of his campaign were proven wrong. Their professional analysts, with years of political experience, had not believed an outcome like this was possible. MSNBC's Joe Scarborough explained, "This election was an earthquake, unlike any earthquake I've seen before . . . it just came out of nowhere."[159] Rachel Maddow, another MSNBC anchor, said to the American people with a deep sigh, "You're awake, by the way; you're not having a terrible, terrible dream. Also, you're not dead, and you haven't gone to hell. This is your life now; this is our election now, this is us, this is our country. It's real."[160] Perhaps one of the most vicious comments about the outcome came from CNN's Van Jones:

"People have talked about a miracle; I am hearing

---

[159] "Joe: 2016 Election Results A 'Complete Earthquake' | Morning Joe | MSNBC." Video. YouTube. Posted by MSNBC, November 9, 2016.

[160] "MSNBC PRESENTATOR ANNOUNCING THAT TRUMP IS THE NEW PRESIDENT." Video. YouTube. Posted by Metamorphosis Gaming, November 9, 2016.

about a nightmare. It's hard to be a parent for a lot of us. You tell your kids don't be a bully. You tell your kids don't be a bigot. You tell your kids to do your homework and be prepared. And then, you have this outcome; people are putting their children to bed tonight, and they are afraid of breakfast. They don't know how to explain it. This was many things. This was a rebellion against the elites. It was a complete reinvention of politics and polls, but it was also something else. This was a white-lash. This was a white-lash against a changing country. Donald Trump has a responsibility now to come out and reassure people that he is going to be the President of all the people he insulted and offended. When you say you want to take your country back, you have a lot of people who say we are not represented well. We do not want a President that has been elected by throwing away some of us to appeal more deeply to others."[161]

Alongside the left-wing media, talk show hosts such as Stephen Colbert, Jimmy Fallon, John Oliver, and Jimmy Kimmel tried to turn what

---

[161] "Van Jones on a Trump win: This was a white lash." Video. YouTube. Posted by CNN, November 9, 2016.

they thought was a tragedy into a comedy. Yet, no matter how hard they tried, their dislike for the president-elect was too deep. On his late-night talk show, Stephen Colbert shockingly said, "There's no way around this. This is what it feels like when America is made great again. I was really hoping it would feel better cause this succkkkks!"[162] John Oliver on Last Week Tonight had similar commentary: "Now, if you're like me, the implications of this have been hitting you in waves. One minute you're numb, and the next minute you realize that Donald Trump, this man, will soon have access to the nuclear codes!"[163] Besides talk shows, liberal YouTube channels aired their grievances to the people. A left-leaning YouTube channel known as "The Young Turks" had consistently been publishing leftist rhetoric during election season. On election night, the host, Cenk Uygur, made a

---

[162] "Celebrities React to Hillary Losing Election." Video. YouTube. Posted by Mark Dice, November 15, 2016.

[163] Ibid.

colorful remark towards Trump supporters:
"You are this close to giving Trump ultimate power on this planet. Are you insane! You pathetic losers!"[164] The rest of the coverage that night was met with even more uncontrollable yelling.

Alongside the many celebrities and media analysts who attacked Trump, historians offered their thoughts. During this supposed "impending crisis," Americans began looking to historians for answers. They wanted reassurance from people who studied the past that the nation has been through worse times than this. While the majority of historians attempted to calm the fears of the American public, there were some who, just like the left-wing media, attacked Trump. One notable historian who was at the forefront of the so-called Historians on Trump movement was David McCullough. McCullough is a world-renowned American historian known for books

---

[164] "The Young Turks Election Meltdown 2016: From smug to utterly devastated." Video. YouTube. Posted by Dame Pesos, November 13, 2016.

such as *1776*, *John Adams*, and *The Johnstown Flood*. He has achieved impressive accolades, such as being a two-time winner of the Pulitzer Prize and receiving the Presidential Medal of Freedom from President George W. Bush in 2006.[165]

Even before Trump was elected, Mr. McCullough decided to provide his analysis. He calmly explained in an interview, "[Donald Trump] is unwise; he is plainly unprepared, unqualified, and it often seems unhinged. How could we possibly put our future in the hands of such a man?"[166] In July 2016, McCullough, along with 50 other historians and biographers, formed a group known as "Historians on Trump." After Trump was elected, the group started gaining popularity and was the subject of many TV interviews. When asked about his motives for

---

[165] "Presidential Medal of Freedom Awarded to David McCullough." Vineyard Gazette. Last modified December 7, 2006.

[166] Anstey, Evan. "Historians warn about a Trump Presidency." WIVB4.com. Last modified August 2, 2016.

starting this movement, McCullough's answer was, "I was outraged by the behavior of the candidate . . . When I think of the kind of people we've had as President of the United States and wonder why this man is in the running to become President? We've got to speak out!"[167] He went on to say, "We need to recover where we were. Ignorance of history is a form of amnesia . . . We parents and grandparents need to do more to teach our children history to prevent something like this from ever happening again."[168]

It is normal to expect the party on the losing side of an election to have negative things to say regarding the president-elect. In a similar fashion, both president-elects Polk and Trump received criticism from the losing party supporters. Despite this rhetoric, however, Americans ultimately accepted the results of these two elections. As former Fox News anchor Megyn Kelly summarized, "That's one of the

---

[167] "McCullough and 'The American Spirit.'" Video. YouTube. Posted by WGBH News, May 8, 2017

[168] Ibid., "The American Spirit"

things that makes us great. We go through this electoral process, we get battered and bruised, but at the end of it, we do accept the result. People will fight on policy, positions, language, and statements, but we all share the same basic core values as Americans, and that is what all of us should focus on."[169]

---

[169] "Megyn Kelly Comments on Election Results." Video. YouTube. Posted by LIVE KellyandRyan, November 9, 2016.

Chapter 11: Presidencies of Nationalism

The presidential election was decided, and both Polk and Trump waited for Inauguration Day when each would officially become president of the United States. In preparation, both men developed their nationalistic agendas.

Since Texas had been annexed three days before Polk took office, Polk's agenda excluded it; however, it did contain:

- The acquisition of the Oregon Territory from Great Britain,
- The acquisition of California,
- The reestablishment of the Independent Treasury, and
- The reduction of tariff rates.[170]

To accomplish this plan, Polk would need a

---

[170] Sellers, Charles. *James K. Polk, Continentalist, 1843-1846*. Princeton, N.J.: Princeton University Press, 1966. 213.

Cabinet. As with every presidential Cabinet, he chose members who were loyal to him and his political agenda. Because he had years of political experience as a member and speaker of the House of Representatives and the governor of Tennessee, he knew many politicians who were capable of filling his Cabinet positions. Those who became members of Polk's presidential Cabinet were either close friends or loyal supporters of his policies delineated during the 1844 campaign. Notably, Polk also chose Cabinet members from different geographic regions, for he wanted a Cabinet that would represent each of the major states and regions of the Democratic Party— New York, Pennsylvania, New England, Virginia, the deep South, and Tennessee.[171] Polk needed to have a balance between geography, ideology, and personal temperament in his Cabinet; otherwise, the administration would not accomplish

---

[171] "Polk's Cabinet." Video. YouTube. Posted by Polk Home, August 5, 2013.

anything.[172]

In the office of his Columbia home, Polk pondered the make-up of his cabinet. Early on, he had opted for Pennsylvania Senator James Buchanan as secretary of state. Buchanan was a successful lawyer and congressmen from Pennsylvania who had supported all of Polk's expansionist polices since the start of his campaign.[173]

Despite Buchanan's impressive legal and political background, Polk was fearful that he would use his position to run for president in the next presidential election. To ensure Buchanan's loyalty, Polk demanded that Buchanan promise he would not do this unless he had permission from Polk.[174] This order angered Buchanan and led to many more disagreements between him and President Polk regarding foreign policy. However, despite their differences, Buchanan

---

[172] Merry, *Vast Designs,* 113.

[173] Ibid., 117.

[174] Ibid., "Polk's Cabinet"

proved to be an integral part of the lengthy negotiations between Great Britain regarding the acquisition of the Oregon Territory and Mexico regarding the acquisition of what is known today as the Southwest United States.

With the secretary of state position filled, Polk now looked to fill the position of secretary of the treasury. Polk believed Senator Robert Walker of Mississippi would fit the bill. Like Polk, Walker supported the renewal of the Independent Treasury and advocated for free trade. He was also a fervid expansionist, writing in one report:

"A higher than any earthly power, still guards and directs our destiny, impels us onward, and has selected our great and happy country as a model and ultimate centre of attraction for all the nations of the world."[175]

When it came to appointing a secretary of war, Polk experienced difficulties. He wanted his

---

[175] Robert J. Walker, "Reports as Secretary of the Treasury for Fiscal Year 1846-47," Niles' Register 73 (December 18, 1847): 255.

secretary of war to come from New York, for this would maintain a regional balance among his Cabinet. He eventually chose New Yorker William Marcy for this position. New York politicians such as Martin Van Buren viewed Marcy as a political enemy. As a result, Van Buren strongly opposed the appointment and asked his son, Smith Van Buren, to deliver a letter to Polk regarding his thoughts on the nomination. When the president-elect received the letter, he held it "as nervously as if it had been a pet snake, which he was half disposed to hold on to, and half disposed to throw out the window."[176] Originally, Van Buren had been Polk's friend. Now, he had become his enemy. Although many did not approve of Marcy's nomination, he would play a critical role in the Mexican-American War.

Representing the New England region was George Bancroft as secretary of the navy. Before his nomination, Bancroft was known as one of America's first historians. When appointed as

---

[176] Sellers, *Continentalist,* 201.

secretary of the navy, he was in the process of writing his ten-volume *History of the United States of America.* Aligning with the Manifest Destiny doctrine, Bancroft wrote this motto on the front cover of his first volume: "Westward the star of empire takes its way."[177] As secretary of the navy, Bancroft founded the U.S. Naval Academy in Annapolis, Maryland. In 1846, Polk appointed Bancroft Ambassador to Great Britain, which allowed him to conduct further research for his work *History of the United States of America.*

Polk picked a longtime friend and former classmate at the University of North Carolina, John Mason, to be his attorney general. Mason had a prosperous law career in Virginia and had achieved impressive accolades in both the state legislature and Congress.[178]

By the time all of Polk's Cabinet positions

---

[177] Bancroft, George. *History of the United States of America.* Vol. I.

[178] "Attorney General: John Young Mason." The United States Department of Justice. Last modified July 6, 2017.

were filled, the inauguration was only three days away. On March 3, newspapers issued the program for Inauguration Day. There would be a patriotic 28-gun salute followed by a procession that would escort the president-elect and his wife to the Capitol Building, where the Oath of Office would be administered by Chief Justice of the Supreme Court Roger B. Taney.[179]

At 10:30 A.M. on Inauguration Day, James K. Polk and his wife were picked up from Coleman's Hotel and began their journey to the Capitol building for the Inauguration ceremony. Unfortunately, the weather did not cooperate, for rainstorms lingered throughout the day. However, the spirit of democracy was more robust than the storms, and, although soaked, Americans still came, umbrellas in hand, to the ceremony.

As Polk traveled down Pennsylvania Avenue in a horse-drawn carriage, military bands played lively marches, creating an enthusiastic mood

---

[179] Jones, J. B. "Order of the Inaugural Procession." *The Daily Madisonian* (Washington, DC), March 3, 1845.

amongst the masses. Marshalls, justices of the Supreme Court, congressmen, and ex-presidents were present at the inauguration, ready for the day's events.

The first order of business at any inauguration is the swearing-in of the vice-president. At 11:00, the Senate was officially called to order. The chambers were filled to the brim with enthusiastic spectators, and the arrival of Supreme Court justices and House leaders soon followed. At 11:40, Polk and his Vice-President, George Dallas, entered the Senate Chambers. Five minutes later, the pro tempore of the Senate administered the Oath of Office to George Dallas, officially making him vice-president.[180] The swearing in of the president-elect was 15 minutes away.

After Vice-President Dallas was sworn in, the assembly of senators, along with influential present and past members of Congress, left the chambers and made their way to the east portico

---

[180] Merry, *Vast Designs*, 5.

of the Capitol Building.[181] The first to emerge was the outgoing president, John Tyler, and the president-elect. They stood side by side, with Polk occupying the ceremonial position to the left of soon-to-be ex-President Tyler. Behind the two men were their respective wives, Sarah Childress Polk and Julia Gardiner Tyler.

---

[181] *Inauguration of President Polk. - The oath*. April 19, 1845. Illustration. Library of Congress, Washington, DC.

James K. Polk as President (1846) *National Portrait Gallery/ Public Domain*

Polk's presidential mentor, Andrew Jackson, as a general in the War of 1812 (top) vs. a retired president in 1840 (bottom) *National Portrait Gallery/ Public Domain*

A political cartoon portraying Andrew Jackson (right) and president of the second bank of the United States Nicholas Biddle (left) as boxers, fighting each other during the Bank War (1834) *Library of Congress/ Public Domain*

The consequence of Andrew Jackson's veto of the
national bank charter renewal, The Panic of 1837.
Library of Congress/ Public Domain

The two candidates in the election of 1844. Henry Clay the Whig candidate (right) and James K. Polk the Democratic candidate (left) *Library of Congress/ Public Domain*

A pro-Democrat cartoon (top) and a pro-Whig cartoon (bottom) *Library of Congress/ Public Domain*

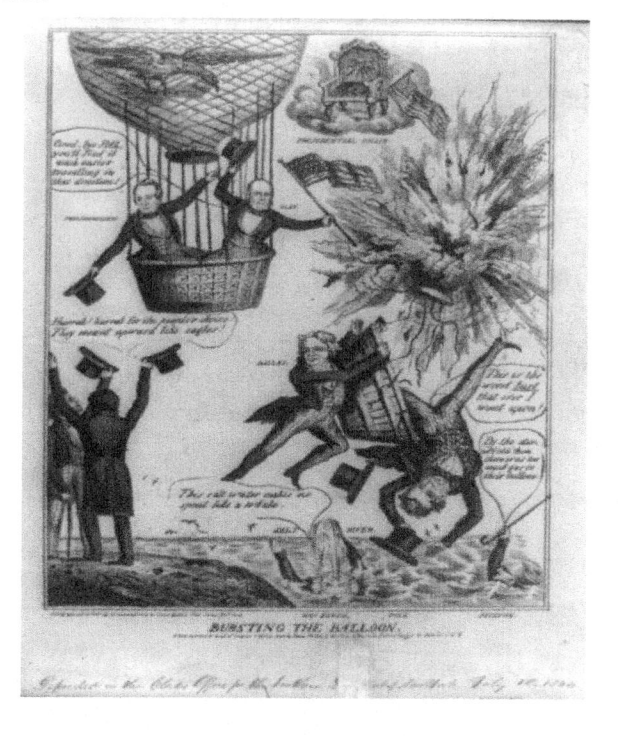

THE GREAT AMERICAN STEEPLE CHASE FOR 1844.

A political cartoon displaying the dysfunctionality of the upcoming 1844 election. *Library of Congress/ Public Domain*

John Tyler, the president without a party, who annexed Texas three days before the inauguration of Polk. *Library of Congress/ Public Domain*

The inauguration of James K. Polk at the East Portico of the Capitol Building. *Library of Congress/ Public Domain*

The new president and vice president from 1845-1849. *Library of Congress/ Public Domain*

A print showing the battles Zachary Talylor was involed in during the Mexican-American War.
Library of Congress/ Public Domain

The victor at the siege of Mexico City, the final battle of the Mexican-American War, Winfield Scott. *National Portrait Gallery / Public Domain*

George Dallas, Polk's vice-president, who cast the deciding vote in the Senate officially enacting the Walker Tariff. *Library of Congress/ Public Domain*

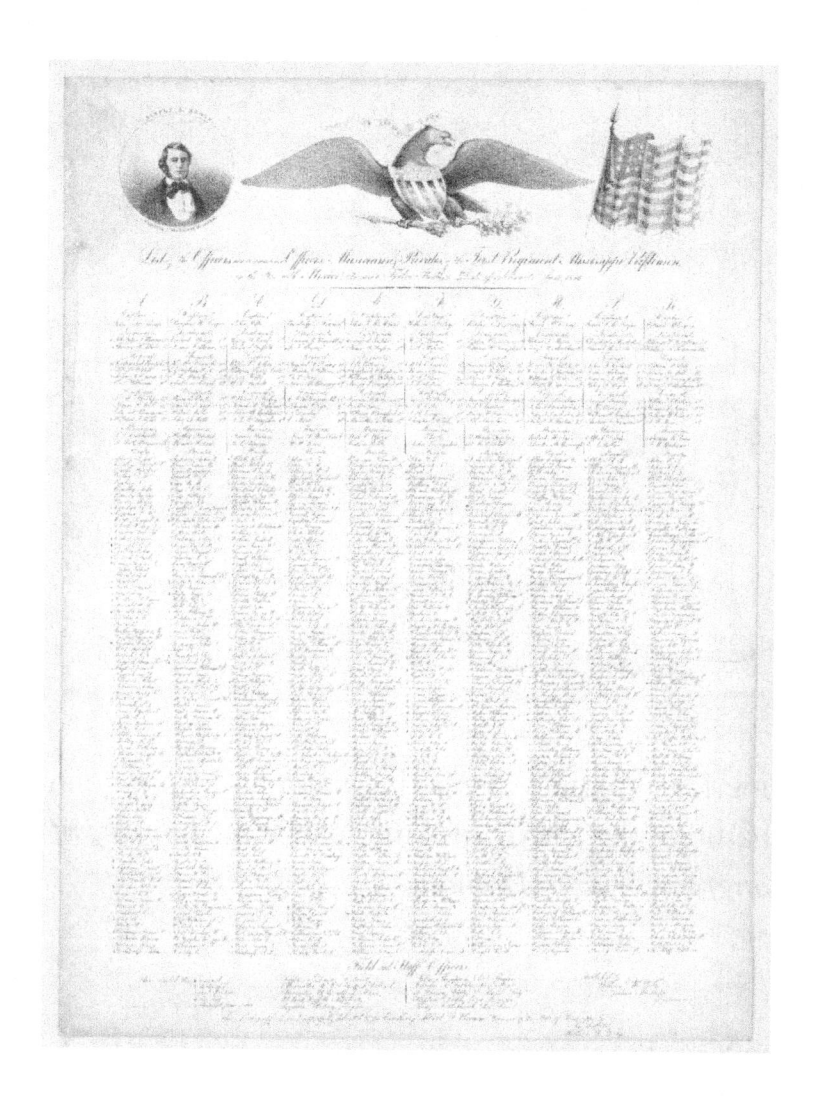

An enlistment sheet showing the sheer amount of men fighting in the first regiment Mississippi riflemen during the Mexican-American War.
Library of Congress/ Public Domain

American soldiers displaying valor and courage in a battle of the Mexican-American War. *Library of Congress/ Public Domain*

A print produced during the election of 1848 showing all of America's past presidents. James K. Polk is the third portrait on the bottom right.
Library of Congress/ Public Domain

It was nearly noon, and Polk would soon become the president. But before taking the Oath of Office, Polk gave his inaugural addresses to the masses during a passing rainstorm. Remembering the teachings of his dying mentor, Polk discussed the core ideals of Jacksonian democracy:

"The Constitution itself, plainly written as it is, the safeguard of our federative compact, the offspring of concession and compromise, binding together in the bonds of peace and union this great and increasing family of free and independent States, will be the chart by which I shall be directed. It will be my first care to administer the government in the true spirit of that instrument, and to assume no powers not expressly granted or implied in its terms."[182]

Taking a page out of Andrew Jackson's book, Polk explained that the federal government would have its power checked, and he warned against bending the literal meaning of the

---

[182] Polk, James K. "Inaugural Address." March 4, 1845. Library of Congress, Washington, DC.

Constitution. He also used the philosophical prophecies of John Locke proclaiming:

> "By the theory of our Government majorities rule, but this right is not an arbitrary or unlimited one. It is a right to be exercised in subordination to the Constitution and conformity to it. One great object of the Constitution was to restrain majorities from oppressing minorities or encroaching upon their just rights. Minorities have a right to appeal to the Constitution as a shield against such oppression."[183]

This principle of government by and for the people was familiar Democratic rhetoric that had originated during the time of Thomas Jefferson. Polk made clear that while he was president, he would act upon the wants and needs of all the people.

Following the Jacksonian rhetoric, Polk briefly outlined his economic and expansionist views, although he did not reveal his four-point agenda. It was not surprising that he denounced a national bank, for he had championed against the

---

[183] Polk. Inaugural Address.

Bank of the United States during the Jackson administration.[184]

When it came to foreign policy, Polk preached expansionist ideals. He celebrated the Manifest Destiny doctrine, stating:

> "Our Union is a confederation of independent States, whose policy is peace with each other and all the world. To enlarge its limits is to extend the dominions of peace over additional territories and increasing millions."[185]

Polk also warned other foreign nations not to intrude on American soil, for this would be a clear violation of the Monroe Doctrine. Fulfilling the wants of his supporters, Polk declared that the acquisition of the whole Oregon Territory was clear and unquestionable, and the settlement of many families in the area supported this notion.[186]

---

[184] Merry, *Vast Designs,* 9.

[185] Polk. Inaugural Address.

[186] Ibid. "Inaugural Address"

After a positive response from the crowd, Justice Taney stepped forward and prepared to administer the presidential Oath of Office. Taney told Polk to place his left hand on "a richly gilt Bible"[187] and raise his right hand. When Taney instructed him to do so, Polk recited 35 words, swearing that he would "preserve, protect, and defend the Constitution of the United States." At that moment, Mr. James Knox Polk became the eleventh president of the United States. With the Oath of Office administered, the president and his wife were escorted to the White House.

One hundred seventy-two years later, the nation would partake in a similar experience with the inauguration of Donald J. Trump. Upon winning the 2016 election, Trump devised a clear agenda that aimed to:

- Repeal all previous executive orders of the Obama administration,
- Build a border wall along the Texas-Mexico border,
- Stop illegal immigration,

---

[187] "Inauguration of The American President," *Illustrated London News*.

- Replace Obamacare,
- Revitalize and strengthen the United States military,
- Provide benefits for veterans,
- Strictly enforce policies that would protect American industries from unfair foreign trade practices,
- Implement a tax cut for middle-class Americans,
- Withdraw the United States from the Iran nuclear deal,
- Win the war against terrorist groups such as ISIS, and
- Provide unemployed Americans with jobs.[188]

    This agenda could not be completed without a Cabinet. When Trump selected his Cabinet members, he chose businessmen, loyal political backers of his agenda, and seasoned military veterans.

    As global issues grew in complexity, the presidential cabinet also expanded. In Polk's time, five cabinet positions needed to be filled. By 2016, there were fifteen positions. The reason for this increase in the number of positions is evident from studying the growth and

---

[188] "Donald Trump Outlines His Presidential Agenda." Video. YouTube. Posted by Fox News, January 22, 2016.

development of the country over time. As the United States became a powerful nation, changes in industry, economics, and homeland security occurred. To address these changes, presidents increased the number of Cabinet positions. The 15 Cabinet positions of today are as follows:

- Secretary of state,
- Secretary of the treasury,
- Secretary of defense,
- Attorney general,
- Secretary of the interior,
- Secretary of agriculture,
- Secretary of commerce,
- Secretary of labor,
- Secretary of health and human services,
- Secretary of housing and urban development,
- Secretary of transportation,
- Secretary of energy,
- Secretary of education,
- Secretary of veterans' affairs, and

- Secretary of homeland security.[189]

Regarding President Trump's Cabinet selections, an important distinction between him and Polk must be made. Because Trump had no political experience, it took time to understand the Washington landscape. As a result, Trump only hired loyal supporters and military personnel, many of whom, like him, had little political experience. This resulted in more frequent changes to Cabinet positions in Trump's first two years in office. His Cabinet today looks much different than it did two years ago. Because of the sheer number of Cabinet positions, we will only be discussing here the cabinet members who played an integral part in the advancement of Trump's major policies.

On November 18, 2016, Trump announced that Jeff Sessions would fill the position of the attorney general. Sessions had served as a

---

[189] Lutz, Eric. "Here is a breakdown of all the Cabinet positions and what they do." Mic. Last modified December 7, 2016

Republican senator in the state of Alabama from 1997–2017, and he was one of the first senators to endorse Trump during his campaign.[190] Over time, conflicts between Sessions and Trump escalated regarding the handling of the Russia Investigation. To prevent further disputes, Sessions resigned as attorney general at Trump's request in 2018. Trump's current attorney general, William Barr, received high honors from law schools such as Columbia University and George Washington University Law School. Barr's tenacity and legal expertise is what ultimately made him an acceptable choice for attorney general. Barr also served as attorney general for President George H. W. Bush from 1991 to 1993.

Trump announced that the secretary of the treasury would be Steve Mnuchin. Mnuchin was a former Goldman Sachs banker and labeled as one of the least controversial appointments of the Trump Cabinet. He served as the Trump

---

[190] "Who's in Trump's Cabinet." Video. YouTube. Posted by CBC News, July 20, 2017.

campaign's finance chair and even advised Trump on potential members of his Cabinet.[191] Mnuchin would fulfill a part of the Trump agenda by promoting a tax cut bill that passed the Republican-controlled Congress in December 2017.

In early December, Trump picked James "Mad Dog" Mattis as his secretary of defense. Although Mattis had served 41 years in the military and garnered many accolades, he did not see eye-to-eye with Trump on issues such as withdrawal from the Iran nuclear deal, the push for no U.S. involvement in Syria, and how to handle climate change.[192] As a result of further disputes over American troops in Syria, Mattis resigned, and Mark Esper replaced him on July 23, 2019.

For the position of secretary of state, Trump originally chose Rex Tillerson, the former CEO of ExxonMobil. Like Trump, Tillerson had no

---

[191] "Steven Mnuchin." Ballotpedia.org.

[192] Ray, Michael. "James Mattis." Encyclopædia Britannica. Last modified September 4, 2019.

political experience, and his tenure as secretary of state would be short. Tillerson clashed with Trump over North Korea and the relocation of the U.S. Embassy in Israel to Jerusalem. Tillerson also accused Trump of being unprepared for a meeting with Russian President Vladimir Putin, Tillerson's so-called pal.[193] In March 2018, Tillerson was fired from his position, making him one of the shortest-serving secretaries of state in recent history. He was replaced by CIA Director Mike Pompeo, who backed Trump's agenda when it came to foreign policy measures with countries such as North Korea and Iran. Pompeo remains in his position.

Despite the changes in personnel made in some of Trump's Cabinet positions, other Cabinet picks remain strong Trump loyalists. Examples include Secretary of Transportation Elaine Chao, Secretary of Agriculture Sonny Perdue, and Secretary of Housing and Urban

---

[193] Phillips, Morgan. "Rex Tillerson: Where is he now?" Fox News. Last modified April 9, 2020.

Development Ben Carson.[194] The fact that some of Trump's primary Cabinet picks were forced to resign or were fired by the President shows that although President Trump was not familiar with the intricacies of the political system, he eventually learned it and picked stronger Cabinet members who would act as his advocates.

Just like Polk's inauguration, the weather during the Trump inauguration was suspect. The day before, a rainstorm had passed over the area, and the skies were still cloudy, dark, and dreary. Many expected that more storms would be coming, but, like Polk supporters, Trump supporters did not let the storms discourage them from witnessing this peaceful transition of power.

After a short service at St. John's Church located in Lafayette Square, the Trump family, along with Vice President-Elect Mike Pence and his wife Karen, entered their separate armored vehicles and were taken to the White House. There, soon-to-be ex-President Barack Obama hosted a tea and coffee reception for the

---

[194] "The Cabinet." whitehouse.gov.

President-Elect and Vice-President and their wives before heading to the Capitol Building for the official swearing in.[195]

Meanwhile, on the west front of the Capitol building, festivities were underway. Tunes such as "My Country, 'Tis of Thee," and "Battle Hymn of the Republic" were playing as Washington elites arrived. Congressmen, senators, and ex-presidents were among the attendees. Members of the president-elect's family, as well as his Cabinet, were present.[196] Despite the tremendous show of American patriotism on Pennsylvania Avenue, protests were occurring in the city district. A far-left militant group known as ANTIFA staged protests during the inauguration. Although protests had also taken place during the respective inaugurations of George W. Bush and Barack Obama, something was different about these

---

[195] "2017 inauguration schedule of events and timeline." Associated Press. Last modified January 20, 2017.

[196] "Donald Trump inauguration day." Video. YouTube. Posted by Guardian News, January 20, 2017.

protests. Throughout the day, ANTIFA members carried signs that read, "Make Racism Great Again" and "No Borders No Nations," and these protests were accompanied with violence and vandalism. In some instances, protesters broke shop windows, violently assaulted police officers, and even set fire to a limousine. Trying to defend themselves, police officers used batons, tear gas, and flash-bang grenades to ward off the protestors, yet their methods seemed to have no effect.[197] It was obvious from these protests the nation was divided over the election of Donald Trump.

The president-elect arrived at the Capitol in preparation for the swearing-in ceremony. As in Polk's day, the vice-president took the Oath of Office first. At 11:35, Associate Justice Clarence Thomas administered the vice-presidential Oath of Office to Mike Pence, making him the 48th vice president of the United States. Twelve minutes later, the presidential Oath of Office was administered to Trump.

When Trump arose from his seat, the

---

[197] Ibid.

American electorate who had voted for him shouted their praise. Trump supporters knew they would face derision, but they also knew they had a president who had their best interests at heart. Chief Justice of the Supreme Court John Roberts instructed the president-elect to recite 35 words and to swear that he would "preserve, protect, and defend the Constitution of the United States," just as Polk had done two centuries ago. Upon the completion of the Oath, Donald John Trump became the 45th president of the United States.

Before partaking in the rest of the day's festivities, President Trump gave his inaugural address to the American people. An important component of his speech included the following statement:

> "Today's ceremony has a very special meaning. Because today, we are not merely transferring power from one administration to another or one party to another. We are transferring power from Washington D.C. and giving it back to you, the people."[198]

---

[198] "Trump Inauguration Speech (FULL)." Video. YouTube. Posted by ABC News, January 20, 2017.

In similar fashion to Polk, President Trump's inaugural speech included elements of patriotism and nationalism. Both presidents called for the government to work in the interests of all the people. Trump promised that every policy passed by his administration would contribute to the prosperity of the American nation. Political underdogs Polk and Trump had earned the presidential prize of a hard-fought battle against the experienced political elites in Washington and were ready to begin work on their political agendas.

Chapter 12: A Change in Expectation and Pride

The respective victories of James Polk and Donald Trump brought a rebirth to America. With these men at the helm of the executive office, the United States entered a period of nationalism and patriotism and the hope for a stronger nation.

By the time news of Polk's victory reached his home in Columbia, Tennessee, he had already started receiving letters from his supporters congratulating him. In his failing health prior to his death, Andrew Jackson wrote this final message to his protégé:

> "I can say in the language of Simeon of old 'Now let thy servant depart in peace,' for I have seen the solution of the liberty of my Country and the perpetuity of our Glorious Union."[199]

---

[199] Remini, Robert V. *Andrew Jackson and the Course of American Democracy, 1833-1845*. Vol. 3. New York: Harper & Row, 1984. 508.

Now that the election was over, the people wanted to return to the growth of American culture, ideals, and reforms. As The *Richmond Enquirer* put it, "We have all become sick and weary of the fierce wrangling of the political arena . . . The noise and the heat of the trial are now over. The people have given in their solemn verdict, to which all patriots will submit."[200]

After Polk's victory, America entered an era of reform. While reform movements such as temperance, women's rights, and abolitionism were popular, America also saw a resurgence in national literature and art. Originally, America had copied the British style. Still, as the country was developing its own national identity, the people realized it was time to implement American ideals into literature and the fine arts. Authors such as James Fenimore Cooper and Washington Irving emerged, who wrote creative stories and portrayed American culture as rugged and individualistic. Around this time, American

---

[200] Ritchie, Thomas. "Political Interregnum." *Richmond Enquirer*, November 12, 1844.

art had evolved in the form of landscapes and vistas painted by institutions such as the Hudson River School. These paintings revealed the pristine territory of the West.

Alongside paintings, American music developed. Previously, American music had consisted of religious tunes based on Puritan ideals. Now, music was shifting away from the austere Puritan doctrine to a folksier style. Songs such as "My Old Kentucky Home" and "Swanee River" were sung in Southern dialects and brought Americans together.

After Polk won the election, American pride was ignited. "The last few years have developed, to a wonderful extent, the genius of the American people," explained the *Richmond Enquirer*. "Literature and the fine arts will receive more votaries. We have already given to the world some of the master spirits of the age, and why should not America, the model of constitutional government, vie with the old world in the more refined accomplishments of social life."[201]

---

[201] Ibid.

Developments in literature and art also brought changes in education. Before the early 1840s, there were few tax-supported schools in the United States. However, with the rise of the Jacksonian Democrats, the common man was able to participate in the democratic process. The majority of this new electorate was illiterate and uneducated; therefore, wealthy Americans needed to put their taxpayer dollars into public education. This would allow the rising electorate to make an educated decision when performing democratic duties such as voting.

As public education flourished, schoolhouses across the United States were built. Many Americans believed the following:

> "All patriots should unite in extending the lights of knowledge to every corner of the [Country]. No people can preserve their freedom, if the dark cloud of ignorance hovers over the land. Let us, then, set to work and organize a system of primary schools, which will provide cheaply and certainly, a more extensive diffusion of knowledge."[202]

---

[202] Ibid.

After the election of James K. Polk, the nation was overcome by an exuberant spirit. As literature and arts flourished, developments in transportation and technology were unifying the United States. The dawn of the railroad and the steamboat stimulated the growth of the American economy. With the building of canals, Americans from different regions of the country could sell their goods to seaports in the North.

These revolutionary improvements in technology and transportation were soon followed by developments in communications. In the early 1840s, Samuel F.B. Morse was in the process of inventing a single-wire telegraph that would transmit correspondence between states at a faster rate. The idea of connecting America through a system of wires correlated directly with the Democratic expansionist doctrine. As Americans moved west, territories that had once been populated with bison became dotted with telegraph wires.

From the perspective of the Democrats, Polk was a catalyst for a grand national rebirth. Polk supporters were hoping for a more powerful America. Perhaps Ralph Waldo Emerson foreshadowed this change when he said:

"America is the country of the future. It is a country of beginnings, of projects, of vast designs and expectations."[203]

With the results of the 2016 election in the history books, Trump supporters had a renewed sense of hope in America. Before Donald Trump became president, many Americans were embarrassed at the state of the country. The Democrats, led by Barack Obama, had not improved the standard of living for working-class Americans. From 2007 to 2015, the median household income dropped from $59,549 to $56,731.[204] Now, Trump would make sure the voices of the ignored were heard. In the streets of

---

[203] Howe, *What Hath God Wrought*, Editor's Introduction, David M. Kennedy. xiii.

[204] "Trump Smashes Obama on Median Household Income." American Liberty Report.

New York City, one Trump supporter said, holding back tears of joy, "I'm going to cry because God saved our country from political corruption and evil."[205] The election of 2016 was not just an election. It was a revolution. The outcome meant hope for a future that would "Make America Great Again," and indeed, it did. Over the next three years, the United States economy would boom. The unemployment rate for Latinos and Blacks would fall to a historic low of 5.1% and 7.5%, respectively.[206] Opportunity zones were set up in the poorer inner cities for the purpose of improving employment of minorities. Average income also rose from $56,731 to $61,937.[207]

---

[205] "Trump 'deplorables' shed tears, rejoice in the streets of NYC." Video. YouTube. Posted by Fox News, November 9, 2016.

[206] "Labor force characteristics by race and ethnicity, 2017." U.S. Bureau of Labor Statistics. Last modified August 2018.

[207] Guzman, Gloria. "New Data Show Income Increased in 14 States and 10 of the Largest Metros." United States Census Bureau. Last modified September 26, 2019.

Imbalances in trade that resulted in middle-class Americans losing their jobs were also addressed. As an initial step, tariffs would be passed on countries such as China, allowing American manufacturing to flourish as it had years ago. Ensuring the well-being of Americans, illegal immigration issues were questioned, and new enforcement procedures were put in place.

This spirit of rebirth and pride in America took hold under both presidents. We can question whether they should be given all the credit, but something in their agendas ignited the flame of American nationalism, pride, and greatness.

Chapter 13: Men of Equal Temperament

Many factors contribute to a successful presidency. The first is the development of an agenda that resonates with the American people. The second is a Cabinet whose members act as advocates for the president to help him fulfill his agenda. Another quality that contributes to a president's success is how he reacts to other people or circumstances when trying to fulfill his agenda—in other words, his temperament.

When Polk was running for office, he promised his supporters he would only serve one term. During his four years in office, Polk accomplished his political agenda, so there was no need to run for a second term in 1848. A contributing factor to his success was his temperament. During his childhood, James K. Polk experienced many adversities, including bladder stones, which led to painful surgery. As a result, he was unable to participate in the activities in which other boys participated. He was also bullied for his ailments. Because of the surgery, Polk was sterile and not able to have children. Living through these setbacks helped Polk acquire the character traits of resilience and grit, which he used to push forward with his agenda, despite the criticism from his adversaries.

Polk excelled at the University of North Carolina, and, although not an intellectual, he developed a work ethic that made him successful not just in school, but also in politics. It was also at the University of North Carolina where Polk developed the brilliant oratory that he would use in his congressional career and presidential campaign. In his time as a member of the House of Representatives, Polk advocated for his mentor, Andrew Jackson, by supporting the elimination of the Second Bank of the United States. In return, Jackson reinforced Polk's character traits of resilience and grit, which would play a significant role in his ability to push his agenda despite harsh criticism.

Throughout his political career, Polk was criticized by members of Congress and the Whig Party. As historian Robert W. Merry once wrote, however:

> "[Polk] understood the forces welling up within the [government] and how they could be harnessed and dominated. He was a master in the art of crafting an effective political message, and he never allowed himself to be deflected from his chosen path by the enmity of his foes or their dismissive regard toward him or their unremitting opposition."[208]

Because of Polk's demeaner, he was able to develop relationships and friendships among the political ranks. The following was written in The *Port-Gibson Correspondent*:

> "[Polk's] calmness and good temper allayed the violence of opposition in a station for which his quickness, coolness, and sagacity eminently qualify him . . . his popularity is owing to the firmness and consistency of his course, his conscientious performance of his duties as a representative, his unwavering patriotism, and his gentlemanly bearing.

---

[208] Merry, *Vast Designs*, 3.

He is calm, conscious, active, decided, and endowed . . ."[209]

During the 1844 presidential campaign, Polk harnessed his character traits of dedication, hard work, and resilience to win over the American public. The Whigs asked the snide question, "Who is James K. Polk?" They thought his nomination was a joke, and their leader, Henry Clay, even said, "Are our Democratic friends serious in the nominations that they have made in Baltimore for president and vice-president!"[210] Alongside their taunting, the Whigs used newspapers such as the *New York Daily Tribune* and the *National Intelligencer* to insult the Democratic candidate, hoping he would eventually drop out. To their surprise, James K. Polk prevailed and was victorious. With Polk in

---

[209] Gage, James A., and Samuel F. Boyd. "James K. Polk, of Tennessee" *Port-Gibson Correspondent* (MS), June 22, 1844.

[210] McNamara, Robert. "Dark Horse Candidate: Origin of the Political Term." ThoughtCo. Last modified October 1, 2019.

the White House, America underwent a patriotic revitalization. Polk's hard work, grit, resilience, and strong will allowed him to complete his agenda.

Unlike Polk, Trump grew up in a wealthy family. Despite the differences in wealth between the Polk and Trump families, Trump did acquire similar values to Polk. His father taught him to persevere through setbacks and the importance of a strong work ethic. At the New York Military Academy and the Wharton School of Finance, Trump competed against the best. This gave him the confidence to run for president, despite the criticism he received.

When Trump took over his family business, he surrounded himself with business associates who shared his values of resilience, perseverance, and commitment. One of these associates was his legal advisor, Roy Cohn. Although many Americans labeled Cohn as abrasive, he reinforced in Trump the importance of defending your position and personal convictions. Additionally, Trump's father taught Donald the temperament needed to be successful, and in

1971, Trump would take over his father's real estate business. Although he experienced bankruptcies, Trump, through his resilience and work ethic, became a successful businessman because he did not allow his failures to dictate his future.

When Trump announced that he was running for president, the Democrats laughed at him the same way the Whigs had disparaged Polk in 1844. Democrats such as Hillary Clinton attacked Trump's lack of political experience as well as temperament, saying, "[Trump] is not just unprepared; he is temperamentally unfit to hold an office that requires knowledge, stability, and immense responsibility."[211] Instead of letting these insults affect him, Trump responded by saying:

> "I think I have a great temperament. I built a tremendous company that is worth many billions of dollars, and I did it in a relatively short amount of

---

[211] Valentine, Janie. "Ballotpedia's Weekly Presidential News Briefing: June 1-5, 20." Ballotpedia News. Last modified June 5, 2020.

time. I have some of the greatest real-estate assets in the world; you don't do that unless you have the right temperament."[212]

When it came to forming relationships, Trump explained, "I get along with Democrats, I get along with Republicans, I get along with everybody, even though I have my enemies."[213]

Although Presidents Polk and Trump were committed to their respective political agendas, they each handled criticism differently. Because Polk had experience in the political arena, having served in the House of Representatives and as governor of Tennessee, he knew how to deal with the negative rhetoric of the Whigs. Therefore, Polk remained calm, despite their ongoing criticism. On the other hand, because Trump lacked political experience, he responded to criticism by attacking his critics. For example, every time a reporter asked him a question that he

---

[212] "Donald Trump: I have a 'great temperament.'" Video. YouTube. Posted by Face The Nation, December 7, 2015.

[213] Ibid.

thought was stupid, he would reply with, "What a stupid question! But I watch you a lot, and you ask a lot of stupid questions!"[214] Trump would act in the same manner when discussing some politicians, giving them labels such as "crooked" and "corrupt." Despite this disparity in delivery, a common trait between the two presidents is their resilience and their commitment to completing their agendas.

If there is one thing to realize about the temperaments of Polk and Trump, it is this: Their experiences taught them the importance of hard work, resilience, and the need to possess a strong will and a fighting spirit. Presidents Polk and Trump had their enemies who believed their agendas and ideas would destroy the country. Despite this, both men, because of their temperaments, remained true to their objectives and focused on fulfilling their policy agendas.

---

[214] "Trump to CNN reporter: What a Stupid Question." CNN. Last modified November 9, 2018.

Chapter 14: Foreign Policy and Tensions with Mexico

A common theme in the respective agendas of Presidents Polk and Trump lies in their foreign policy. The strengthening of America's standing on the world stage was their ultimate goal. To achieve this goal, the presidents needed to challenge the foreign nations that had threatened this objective and the American way of life.

After Polk won the presidential election in November 1844, his victory was interpreted as a mandate to annex Texas. The majority wanted Texas admitted as the 28th state of the Union. The previous president, John Tyler, had tried to pass an annexation treaty with Texas in June of 1844, unfortunately to no avail.

In the final days of his presidency, Tyler again proposed a new annexation treaty that could be passed through a joint resolution of Congress. Instead of a two-thirds majority in the Senate, the treaty only needed to have a simple majority in both houses to become ratified.[215] The Southern Democrats fully supported annexation, yet it would take the Northern Democrats some convincing. Robert Walker, the senator from Mississippi who would later become Polk's secretary of the treasury, made this claim to Northerners: If Texas were not annexed, freed emancipated Blacks from the South would move to the Northern industrial centers where nothing but conflict between Whites and Blacks regarding factory jobs and wages would ensue.[216]

Walker's argument provided Northerners with the reasons why Texas annexation would help the United States as a whole, not just the South. Now, the treaty would go through both houses of Congress smoothly. When it came time for ratification, the new annexation treaty made it through the Democratic-controlled House of Representatives with ease. Yet, the Senate, which

---

[215] Howe, *What Hath God Wrought,* 698.

[216] Hartnett, Stephen, *Democratic Dissent and the Cultural Fictions of Antebellum America,* (Urbana, Ill., 2002), 103-31.

had a narrow Whig majority, would not be so lenient. A group known as the "Conscience" Whigs opposed annexing Texas into the Union because of the slavery expansion agreed to under the Missouri Compromise of 1820. Despite this opposition, the new annexation treaty made it through the House 128 to 98, and barely made it through the Senate, 27 to 25.[217] On March 1, 1845—three days before the inauguration of Polk—Tyler signed the treaty.

With the annexation of Texas completed, the acquisition of the Oregon Territory was next on the agenda. Parts of the Oregon Territory were claimed at one time by four different nations. Two of them, Russia and Spain, bartered away their claims to America in the Adams-Onis Treaty in 1819 and the Russo-American Treaty in 1824.[218] The only two nations left with a territorial interest were Great Britain and America, both of which were vying for complete

---

[217] Howe, *What Hath God Wrought,* 699.

[218] Kennedy, David M., et al. *The American Pageant.* 375.

control over the territory.

Even though America and Great Britain agreed to a joint occupation of Oregon in 1818, the relationship between the two countries was hostile. There was still resentment over the American victories in the Revolutionary War and the War of 1812. The pro-British Hamiltonian Federalists had disappeared and were replaced with the rough, individualistic Jacksonian Democrats. In 1837, the Americans came to the aid of the Canadians during their revolts against the British government. An American steamer *Caroline* carried reinforcements and supplies to aid the Canadians. On the night of December 29, British militiamen attacked the *Caroline*, set fire to the ship and sank it in the middle of the Niagara River.[219] Six days later, news of the *Caroline*'s sinking reached Washington, and instead of declaring war, President Martin Van Buren decided to remain neutral in the conflict between Canada and the British. Although Americans accepted Van Buren's decision,

---

[219] Howe, *What Hath God Wrought,* 518.

tensions between America and Great Britain ran high.

Despite the hostility, Americans continued settling in the Oregon Territory. Fur trappers and farmers were among the first settlers to cross the Rockies, and they chose to settle near the Willamette Valley, a fertile area south of the Columbia River with abundant timber resources.[220] Westward pioneers viewed the Willamette Valley as the Promised Land. This was especially true for farmers from the Mississippi Valley, who wanted to escape the region's economic depression and malaria.[221] Fur trappers representing the American Fur Company also settled in the Oregon Territory to profit from the lucrative fur trade. As more fur trappers arrived in Oregon, the American Fur Company's profitability increased. A British Fur Company operating as the Hudson Bay Company started to lose its influence and control over the Oregon

---

[220] Ibid., 712.

[221] Ibid.

region.

As with many territorial conquests, Native American tribes felt the full effects of colonization. This was no exception with the settlement of Oregon. While the British viewed the natives as customers and supplied them with various pelts and firearms, the Americans wanted to confiscate lands and even go to war with the natives.[222] While the majority of settlers disliked the natives, missionaries tried to bring Christianity to them. These missionaries had an influential impact on the growth of the region, establishing institutions that became important in the settlement of the Oregon Territory. By the end of 1844, about 5,000 Americans lived in the Oregon country compared to just 700 British subjects.[223] As a result of winning the population race, expansionist Americans wanted Oregon for

---

[222] Merk, Frederick. *The Oregon Question: Essays in Anglo-American Diplomacy and Politics*. Cambridge, Belknap Press of Harvard UP, 1967. 234-54.

[223] Dary, David. *The Oregon Trail: An American Saga*. New York: Alfred A. Knopf, 2004.

themselves.

The process of acquiring the entire Oregon Territory from Great Britain was risky. Polk supporters who rallied around the phrase "Fifty-four Forty or Fight!" wanted the boundary line to extend to 54° 40' latitude. The British, on the other hand, wanted the existing 49th parallel boundary extended to the west, at which point the boundary would follow the Columbia River to the Pacific Ocean. With these competing interests in mind, President Polk began negotiations.

As negotiations were underway, Polk kept a close eye on the British government. The last thing the president wanted was a war with powerful Great Britain over the Northwest territory. Therefore, while seeming to demand all of Oregon, Polk was willing to compromise to prevent war. If a peaceful settlement were made, the British would not come to Mexico's aid during the Mexican-American War.[224] Compromising over the territory had its difficulties, as the majority of Democrats who

---

[224] Ibid., 717.

felt entitled to the Annexation of Texas also felt entitled to acquire the entire Oregon Territory. In an attempt to please his supporters, Polk appointed Louis McLane as a U.S. envoy to Great Britain. The British Foreign Office sent Richard Pakenham to Washington. When Pakenham left for America, he received two sets of instructions: stick firmly to British interests and refer any American proposal back to London immediately.[225]

In July, 1845, the Polk administration offered to divide the Oregon Territory at the 49th parallel as an initial proposition. Initially, Pakenham outright refused the proposal, for he did not want the British to let go of the valuable resources along the Columbia River. Furious, President Polk took action and asked Congress to pass an act giving Great Britain the following ultimatum: the joint occupation of the Oregon Territory would be no more if a solution to the territory dispute was not given within a period of one

---

[225] Pletcher, David M. *The Diplomacy of Annexation: Texas, Oregon, and the Mexican War*. Columbia, U of Missouri P, 1973. 242-43.

year.[226] On April 23, 1846, Congress enacted the act attached with an amendment encouraging a final decision on the Oregon question. In response, the British proposed the 49th parallel after realizing the Columbia River did not provide as many resources as the St. Lawrence river did further north. Polk would break his promise to his supporters by not acquiring the land at the 54° 40' parallel because British firmness on the issue forced him to do so. On February 21, Secretary of State James Buchanan received a dispatch from U.S. envoy McLane saying that 30 British warships were en route for North America. For several days, Polk and his cabinet planned out their response. Polk knew the United States could not defend itself against the mighty British Empire with its impressive flotillas and organized regiments. Even though Polk had an agenda to complete, the safety of the American people always came first, and therefore, compromise was necessary. Five days later, Polk instructed McLane to assure the

---

[226] Howe, *What Hath God Wrought*, 719.

British that the United States would be willing to accept the boundary proposal.[227]

The Oregon treaty swiftly passed through the Senate 38 to 12. On June 18, 1846, Polk sent it to the British government in London, and 10 days later, the Oregon question had an answer: The United States had control of the Oregon Territory up to the 49th parallel. Although Polk had failed to adhere to the cries of his supporters for "Fifty-four Forty or Fight!", he had managed to peacefully acquire Oregon without a shot fired. To the Polk administration, this represented a foreign policy victory.

While Polk negotiated with the British, a war between Mexico and the United States was underway. Polk's personal objective was to acquire California from Mexico. Although Polk campaigned on a platform to acquire Texas and Oregon, he did not have the same mandate when acquiring California. Yet, it was becoming evident that the Mexican government could not hold on to California forever. In the 1830s, Mexicans rebelled against President Antonio

---
[227] Ibid., 721.

López de Santa Anna's dictatorial regime, which led to his exile to Cuba. With the Mexican army concentrated in Mexico City, California was open to settlement, and many nations wanted the territory.

Many Americans during the 1820s and 30s were attracted to California's fertile land. Beginning in 1841, hundreds of settlers organized themselves in wagon trains, bound for California. While many settlers were eager and enthusiastic to start a new life in the territory, the trail they journeyed on was dangerous. Disease such as malaria could be contracted at any time, and Native American attacks were frequent. Many westward pioneers feared crossing the Sierra Nevada. If settlers waited until winter, the snow from the mountains would halt the journey, causing many to resort to cannibalism to avoid starvation. Despite the arduous journey, many westward pioneers settled in California.

Polk was willing to do whatever it took to acquire the California territory. Still, haste was necessary, as rumors were spreading about Britain negotiating with Mexico to acquire the region. One of Polk's first plans for annexing California was to buy it from Mexico. However, this action would prove futile due to the hostility that had arisen over the recent Texas annexation. After President of the Lone Star Republic Anson Jones received the joint resolution treaty from Congress in 1845, the Texan Congress ratified it in Austin, and a state constitution was drafted and sent to the United States Congress in Washington for approval. Even though Congress accepted the state constitution in December, President Jones did not turn over legal authority to the federal government until February 1846.[228] Although the issue of statehood was resolved, the question of state boundaries was not. The Mexican government considered the southernmost border of Texas to end at the Nueces River, a border that had been established since Texas became an independent nation in 1836. Polk and other Democratic expansionists, on the other hand, believed the southernmost border of Texas ended at the Rio Grande. From the day Polk took office,

---

[228] Ibid., 732.

he, as well as members of his administration, made clear that the boundary was the Rio Grande, and he would attack the Mexicans if they encroached on the territory.

On June 15, 1845, Polk ordered Major General Zachary Taylor, along with 4,000 men, to approach as close to the Rio Grande as possible in case of a Mexican skirmish. Upon receiving the order, Taylor stationed his men at Corpus Christi by the mouth of the Nueces River.[229]

Although relations between America and Mexico were tense, Polk attempted to negotiate. His main goal was to acquire California from Mexico. If he had to go to war with Mexico, then he wanted it to be on a small scale so that the United States could quickly recover. He decided to send Louisiana Congressman John Slidell, a fervid supporter of the president during the 1844 election, to Mexico City with the following instructions: Make clear to the Mexican government that the Texas-Mexico border is at the Rio Grande, and offer $25 million for

---

[229] Pletcher, *Diplomacy of Annexation*, 255-56.

California and any other territories to the east. Polk also demanded that Mexico pay back the $3 million in debt it owed to the United States for damages caused during the Texas Revolution.[230] As Slidell would soon find out, the Mexican government was not so willing to accept these terms.

From the Mexican standpoint, selling California was unthinkable. However, in the same way that the British despised the United States, the United States hated Mexico and showed no empathy towards the Mexican government. While Polk was willing to compromise with the British when it came to Oregon, he would not compromise with Mexico when it came to California. He would stop at nothing to acquire California, whether it be through peace or war.

When Slidell arrived in Mexico City, the Mexican government was in complete disarray. Mexican President José Joaquín Antonio de Herrera had been replaced by Mariano Paredes,

---

[230] Howe, What Hath God Wrought, 734.

FOREIGN POLICY AND TENSIONS WITH MEXICO

who refused to receive Slidell, making his journey a waste of time. After the rejection, Slidell explained to Polk, "A war would probably be the best mode of settling our affairs with Mexico."[231] By the end of December, Slidell was on a ship en route for the United States, returning home empty-handed.

In January 1846, the news reached Washington that the Slidell mission had failed. This prompted the Polk administration to order General Taylor and his 4,000 men to march from Corpus Christi to the Rio Grande. This executive order was a clear violation of Mexican boundary rights. Many Whigs and even some Democrats in Congress believed Polk was insane for carrying out this order. While many presidents had taken advice from their congressmen, Polk refused to. He knew what his supporters wanted, and as president of the United States, he believed it was his duty to fulfill America's Manifest Destiny.

As Taylor led his men through the disputed Mexican territory, members of his regiment

---

[231] Pletcher, *Diplomacy of Annexation,* 357.

disagreed with the notion of war with Mexico. Among these people was Colonel Ethan Allen Hitchcock. Hitchcock was an experienced military commander who had served as Taylor's aide during the war. In March, 1846, he wrote the following in his diary:

> "I have said from the start that the United States are the aggressors . . . We have not one particle of right to be here . . . It looks as if the government sent a small force on purpose to bring on the war, so as to have a pretext for taking California and as much of this country as it chooses, for, whatever becomes of this army, there is no doubt of a war between the United States and Mexico."[232]

Men like Colonel Hitchcock believed the Mexican-American War was a conflict that should not have taken place. In its current state, the Mexican government was financially unstable, ill-prepared for a major war, and had no

---

[232] Hitchcock, Ethan Allen, and W. A. Croffut. *Fifty Years in Camp and Field: Diary of Major-General Ethan Allen Hitchcock, U.S.A.* New York, G.P. Putnam's Sons.

European allies.[233] The country of Mexico, no matter the actions it took, was fighting a losing battle, for the United States was more unified and powerful.

Meanwhile, back in Washington, Polk and his cabinet began drafting a declaration of war, for Polk had received correspondence from General Taylor saying that 1,600 Mexican cavalrymen led by Commander Mariano Arista had found out about the American invasion, and an attack was expected at any moment. On May 9, 1846, Polk would ask Congress to declare war on two counts: refusal to accept the proposal offered by Slidell regarding California and failure to keep up payments on the debt owed to the United States. On the same day, Polk received news that the Mexican forces had crossed the Rio Grande and attacked the Americans, resulting in 16 Americans killed or wounded.[234] With this information in mind, Polk revised his war

---

[233] Howe, *What Hath God Wrought,* 740.

[234] Kennedy, David M., et al. *The American Pageant.* 381.

message:

> "The cup of forbearance had been exhausted even before the recent information from the frontier of the [Rio Grande]. But now, after reiterated menaces, Mexico has passed the boundary of the United States, has invaded our territory and shed American blood upon the American soil . . . I invoke the prompt action of Congress to recognize the existence of the war, and to place at the disposal of the Executive the means of prosecuting the war with vigor, and thus hasting the restoration of peace."[235]

When Polk's war message was read aloud to the House of Representatives, it was met with opposition. Even though the House had a Democratic majority, they debated with the Whigs over the necessity of a war with Mexico. Luther Severance, a Whig representative from Maine, explained, "It is on Mexican soil that blood has been shed. The Mexicans should be honored and applauded for their manly

---

[235] Memorandum, "Hostilities by Mexico," May 11, 1846. James K. Polk Papers. Library of Congress, Washington, DC.

resistance."[236] Despite the opposition, the war measure passed in the House.

In the Senate, the war declaration was met with opposition from not only the Whigs, but the Democrats as well. While the majority of Democrats wanted war with Mexico, some senators, including John C. Calhoun of South Carolina, believed that territorial acquisition of California would harm the sectional balance between the North and South regarding the slavery issue. Some Northern Democratic senators also opposed the war, saying that the Mexican government was in the right and the United States was in the wrong.[237] In the end, the war measure made it through the Senate, and President Polk officially declared war on May 13, 1846.

When one looks at the advantages and disadvantages of both countries heading into the Mexican-American War, it was clear who would

---

[236] Sellers, *Continentalist*, 794.

[237] Howe, *What Hath God Wrought*, 743.

emerge victorious. While Mexico had power in numbers, the United States had the advantage of a powerful artillery.[238] The American generals knew that the Mexican army was not ready for war because of the economic problems plaguing the country, as well as the country's lack of resources.[239] As a result, America believed that this war would be short, easy, and inexpensive. However, this would prove not to be the case.

Even though the United States had experienced artillerymen, the Mexican army, although small by European standards, was more substantial than that of the United States. In the majority of battles, America was outnumbered. However, with the internal disputes occurring in Mexico City, Mexican troops were tired, for the Mexican government had been using the military to end violent internal protests. The patriotic American army displayed effective military leadership, sharp knowledge of military strategy, and, most importantly, perseverance and

---

[238] Ibid., 745.

[239] Ibid., 749.

courage.

The majority of battles fought during the Mexican-American War were American victories. The military prowess of Major General Zachary Taylor contributed to American victories at Palo Alto, Resaca de la Palma, and Monterey. As the fighting was underway in southern Mexico, President Polk dispatched General Stephen W. Kearny to the southwest to ensure that the territories of California and New Mexico were free from Mexican control. Persuading the 3,000 Mexican troops to withdraw, Kearny marched unopposed into Santa Fe on August 18, 1846.[240] After capturing Santa Fe, Kearny advanced to California, where he met John C. Frémont. Frémont and his men managed to overthrow the Mexican rule in California and established their own government in the form of the Bear Flag Republic.[241] With successes in the

---

[240] Encyclopedia Britannica, The Editors Of. "Stephen Watts Kearny." Encyclopedia Britannica. Last modified October 27, 2019.

[241] Kennedy, David M., et al. *The American Pageant*. 284.

Southwest, President Polk decided to negotiate with Mexico one last time.

While the war raged, Mexico's overthrown dictator, Antonio López de Santa Anna, wished to return to Mexico. To accomplish this, he made an offer to Washington: If the United States arranged for him to return to Mexico, the former dictator would seize power again and make peace.[242] The president accepted Santa Anna's offer. Unfortunately, however, instead of complying with the promises made to the United States, Santa Anna broke every promise he had made to Polk and rallied Mexicans to fight against the oppressive United States.

In February 1847, General Taylor and his feeble force of men defeated 20,000 Mexican troops at the Battle of Buena Vista. With this victory procured, America experienced a massive morale boost that resulted in victory after victory for the rest of the war. Delivering the final blow in the war was Major General Winfield Scott. Scott was one of the greatest generals of his time.

---

[242] Howe, *What Hath God Wrought,* 766.

In addition to the Mexican-American War, Scott had served in the War of 1812 and later for the Union in the Civil War. Although Scott was an impressive military figure, he had earned the unfavorable nickname "Old Fuss 'n' Feathers" for his strict military discipline and uniform. Despite the criticism he received, Scott ran an aggressive military campaign that was en route to capture the government epicenter in Mexico City. After his victory at Veracruz, Scott and his men advanced on to the Mexican capital. Along the journey, Scott's army experienced rough terrain and skirmishes from Mexican forces at Molino del Rey and Chapultepec. Yet, Scott was successfully able to take over Mexico City on September 15, 1847. The United States emerged victorious in the Mexican-American War.

With victory secured, Polk decided it was time to put a peaceful end to the conflict. The president sent Chief Clerk of the State Department Nicholas P. Trist to negotiate with the Mexican government. In the beginning, Trist's negotiations were going nowhere, and Polk concluded that Trist should resign from his position. Secretary of State Buchanan sent a letter to Trist on October 6, 1847, instructing him to return "at the first safe opportunity."[243] When Trist received the letter on November 16, he decided to ignore the measure and carry on negotiations as planned. This ended up being the right course of action, for Trist was able to successfully negotiate the Treaty of Guadalupe Hidalgo on February 2, 1848. After the signing of the treaty, Mexico agreed to recognize the Texas boundary at the Rio Grande, and they ceded to the United States what is now considered the American Southwest. From the Mexican Cession, the states of California and Nevada were procured, along with parts of New Mexico and Arizona. The United States agreed to pay $15 million for the land.[244] Although Polk felt bitterness towards Trist for failing to follow his executive order, he sent the treaty to the

---

[243] Robert Brent, "Nicholas P. Trist and the Treaty of Guadalupe Hidalgo," *Southwestern Historical Quarterly* 57 (1954): 454-74.

[244] Kennedy, David M., et al. *The American Pageant.* 385.

Senate where, despite Whig opposition, it was passed 38–14. James K. Polk had accomplished the second part of his agenda, annexing California.

Even though the Mexican-American War was short, it had major repercussions. America's total land mass had increased by one-third, and the nation's Manifest Destiny was fulfilled. Most American casualties occurred not from battle but disease. By the end of the war, 12,518 Americans had died on the battlefield or from diseases such as smallpox. [245] Even though victory had been declared, James K. Polk would receive criticism from politicians for the consequences of his actions.

Shifting to Donald Trump's foreign policy, his doctrine and Polk's have similarities. Both presidents believed in the need to put America first. When reporters ask questions about Trump's foreign policy agenda, he explains, "My foreign policy will always put the interests of the

---

[245] Winders, Richard Bruce. *Mr. Polk's Army: The American Military Experience in the Mexican War*. College Station, Texas A & M UP, 1997.

American people and American security above all else. It has to be first, has to be. That will be the foundation of every single decision that I will make."[246] During his campaign, Trump criticized the actions of the Obama administration, saying:

> "The foreign policy of the current administration is a total disaster. It has no vision, no purpose, no direction, and no strategy. If President Obama's goal had been to weaken America, he could not have done a better job."[247]

Upon taking office, Trump unveiled his *National Security Strategy,* which was intended to "protect the American people, preserve their way of life, promote their prosperity, preserve peace through strength, and advance American influence in the world."[248] In the plan, Trump

---

[246] Beckwith, Ryan Teague. "Read Donald Trump's 'America First' Foreign Policy Speech." TIME. Last modified April 27, 2016.

[247] Ibid.

[248] Trump, Donald J. National Security Strategy of the United States of America. December 2017. 1.

outlined the countries doing the most harm to American prosperity. While Polk only dealt with Britain and Mexico, Trump had to deal with not just Mexico but also China, Russia, North Korea, and the Middle East.[249]

One of the first countries that Trump needed to deal with was Mexico. At the start of the campaign, Trump promised his supporters, "I will build a great, great wall on our southern border. And I will have Mexico pay for that wall."[250] By building a wall along the U.S.-Mexico border, Trump would be protecting the American way of life from rapists, drug cartels, and immigrants who were crossing the border illegally. Throughout the campaign, Trump made this statement clear: "When Mexico sends its people, they are not sending their best. They are sending people that have a lot of problems, and they are bringing those problems to the United

---

[249] Ibid.

[250] Valverde, Miriam. "How Trump plans to build, and pay for, a wall along U.S.-Mexico border." PolitiFact. Last modified July 26, 2016.

States. They're bringing drugs, they're bringing crime, and they're rapists."[251] Out of every promise Trump made, none received more recognition than the border wall. At Trump rallies, it was not uncommon to see Trump supporters shout "Build that wall!" followed by the campaign slogan "Make America Great Again."

Five days after taking the Oath of Office, Trump signed an executive order to begin construction on a 2,000-mile-long border wall along the U.S.-Mexico border. Later that same day, Mexican President Enrique Peña Nieto gave his opinion:

> "I regret and disapprove of the decision by the United States to continue with the construction of the wall, which will far from unite us, it will divide us. Mexico does not believe in walls. I have said time and

---

[251] "Donald Trump doubles down on calling Mexicans 'rapists.'" Video. YouTube. Posted by CNN, June 25, 2015.

FOREIGN POLICY AND TENSIONS WITH MEXICO

time again, Mexico will not pay for any wall."[252]

While relations between President Nieto and President Trump seemed tense at that moment, the two countries were willing to work together. Although Trump believed in putting America first, he was ready to engage in constructive dialogue with other countries to resolve differences. On the morning of January 27, two days after the executive order for the border wall was signed, Presidents Trump and Nieto had a telephone call discussion. During the call, both presidents recognized their differences on issues such as the border wall; however, unlike President Polk, both agreed to work these differences out and compromise.[253] Although Trump's objective was to ensure the prosperity of the American people, he was willing to engage in

---

[252] Evans, Natalie, Christopher Bucktin, and Scott Campbell. "Mexican president CANCELS meeting with Donald Trump.

[253] "Joint Statement on U.S.-Mexico Relations." Whitehouse.gov. Last modified January 27, 2017.

dialogue to resolve differences, a striking difference from President Polk's approach when it came to Mexico.

Besides the border wall, The North American Free Trade Agreement (NAFTA) contributed to a high trade deficit between the United States and Mexico. Before NAFTA began, the United States had a trade surplus with Mexico of over $1 billion. When Trump took office, the United States had a trade deficit of $58.8 billion.[254] Trump despised NAFTA because, although it benefited Mexico and Canada, it contributed to American unemployment in the United States. As a result, Trump decided to take action. On November 30, 2018, the United States, Mexico, and Canada signed the United States-Mexico-Canada Agreement (USMCA). This agreement created "a more balanced, reciprocal trade that supports high-paying jobs for Americans while continuing to grow the North American

---

[254] "What would a trade war with Mexico mean for the U.S.?" Video. YouTube. Posted by Fox Business, January 26, 2017.

economy."[255] After dealing with Mexico, Trump turned to foreign policy issues overseas.

In his *National Security Strategy,* Trump described China as "a challenge to American power, influence, and interests. The country is determined to make economies less free and less fair, to grow their militaries, and to control information and data to repress their societies and expand their influence."[256] Trump promised his supporters he would deal with China, which was taking away American jobs and contributing to the destruction of the American manufacturing sector.[257] Although Trump criticized China, he knew they were putting their own country first. Previous administrations who chose not to put America first allowed the trade deficit of

---

[255] "United States-Mexico-Canada Agreement." *United States Trade Representative*, ustr.gov/trade-agreements/free-trade-agreements.

[256] Trump, Donald J. National Security Strategy of the United States of America. December 2017. 2.

[257] "Trump visits China." Video. YouTube. Posted by ABC News, November 8, 2017.

countries such as China to increase. President Trump, a man of the people, was determined to see to it that China treated its American partner fairly.

In early November 2017, President Trump traveled to Beijing to engage in negotiations with Chinese President Xi Jinping regarding trade and other domestic issues. While Trump attacked China during his campaign, he seemed to show a gentler tone while in Beijing. During his visit, Trump and Xi agreed to deals worth a total of $253.5 billion USD.[258] The summit between the president of the United States and the president of China paved the way for trade discussions between the two nations. China also agreed with the United States that North Korea should demilitarize, and intellectual property of U.S. companies should be protected. These relations led to the start of a trade deal with China, with Phase One being signed on January 15, 2020. The deal included intentions to discuss "the

---

[258] "China, US sign record $253.5 bln deals during Trump visit." Video. YouTube. Posted by CGTN, November 9, 2017.

elimination of intellectual property theft and forced technology transfers as well as increased Chinese purchases of U.S. goods."[259] Although these negotiations have not been completely successful, the preliminary discussions have moved intellectual property and trade issues to the forefront—a positive direction.

Unlike Mexico and China, where discussions were based on fairer trade agreements and reductions in trade deficits, disagreements with Russia were mostly based on military issues.[260] Trump felt the need to establish better relations with Russia, as the country's nuclear capacity was the most existential threat to the United States. This threat surfaced in the final presidential debate of the 2016 election, when Trump articulated, "[The United States] is in very serious trouble. Because [Russia] is a country

---

[259] Pramuk, Jacob. "Trump signs 'phase one' trade deal with China in push to stop economic conflict." CNBC. Last modified January 15, 2020.

[260] Trump, Donald J. National Security Strategy of the United States of America. December 2017. 25.

with tremendous numbers of nuclear warheads, 1,800 by the way . . ."[261] One of the conspiracy theories that circulated during 2016 was that Russia meddled in the presidential election, helping Donald Trump get elected. This scheme conjured up by the Democratic Party was eventually revealed to be a hoax, as no evidence was presented by the investigation led by Robert Muller. As President Trump summarized, "It was a witch hunt."[262]

Surprisingly, when news of the election results became known in Russia, many Russians were happy for the United States. Dmitri Drobnitski, a Russian journalist for *LifeNews*, said:

> "I congratulate the American people with their will and their democracy, as well as their strength and courage. This is not only a victory for the Americans

---

[261] "Donald Trump and Hillary Clinton on 'Putin's puppet.'" Video. YouTube, posted by CBS News, October 19, 2016.

[262] Singman, Brooke. "Trump says 'Russian Witch Hunt' costing $10M, 'no Collusion' one year later." Fox News. Last modified May 15, 2018.

who defended their democracy against the liberal globalist elite. This is a victory that the American people brought to the whole world."[263]

President Putin, accused of using Trump as a puppet, expressed similar sentiments:

"A big plus of President Trump is that he aspires to fulfill his promises, especially those given to the American people. Generally, after an election, some leaders quickly forget what they have promised to their people. But Trump does not."[264]

This respect for President Trump made it easier to hold discussions between the two countries. On July 7, 2017, both presidents shook hands at the G20 Summit, where discussions

---

[263] "Russians celebrate Donald Trump's US election victory." Video. YouTube, posted by The Telegraph, November 9, 2016,

[264] "Russian President Vladimir Putin Invites President Donald Trump To Moscow: 'Be My Guest.'" Video. YouTube. Posted by NBC News, July 27, 2018.

about creating better relations were held.[265]

On July 16, 2018, Presidents Trump and Putin would meet again in Helsinki, Finland, to further discuss ways to improve the relationship between the United States and Russia. Topics such as issues in the Middle East, the annexation of Crimea, and ways to improve the cyber security of both countries were discussed. [266] Trump continues to believe that improving relations between the United States and Russia through open dialogue is important. His attention has since turned to North Korea.

Trump made a serious effort to resolve the nuclear ambitions of North Korea that threatened the safety of America and her allies. The main policy issue for President Trump regarding North Korea was the country's ambitions to develop nuclear weapons that could eventually reach the United States mainland and, in the nearer term,

---

[265] "HISTORIC MEETING: President Trump and Vladimir Putin First Meeting." Video. YouTube, posted by CNN, July, 7 2017.

[266] Simon, Abigail. "Read a Transcript of Trump and Putin's Joint Press Conference." TIME. Last modified July 31, 2018.

threaten its Indo-Pacific allies.[267] President Trump promised his supporters he would engage in peaceful negotiations with North Korea regarding denuclearization.

In March, 2018, the Trump administration began making plans for a historic summit between the United States and North Korea. If a summit between these two countries were to take place, Trump would be the first president to meet with the North Korean president. Although there were rumors about the summit being called off, it was eventually made official, and both presidents agreed to meet in Singapore that summer. On June 12, 2018, Kim Jun Un and Donald J. Trump held their historic summit at the Capella Hotel in Sentosa, Singapore. During the summit, both presidents signed a joint statement agreeing to pursue security guarantees for North Korea, new peaceful relations, the denuclearization of the Korean Peninsula, and follow-up negotiations

---

[267] Trump, Donald J. National Security Strategy of the United States of America. December 2017. 36.

between high-level officials.[268] After the summit concluded, President Trump remarked, "I think our whole relationship with North Korea and the Korean Peninsula is going to be a different situation than it has in the past."[269] Although negotiations were subsequently called off, many believe that the groundwork has been laid for further discussion.

The Middle East has long been an area where the American military was bogged down in many unwinnable skirmishes, with no easy policy solutions. Terrorist groups such as ISIS had created their own caliphates out of parts of Syria and Iraq. Because of these circumstances, a large influx of refugees was coming into Europe. Terrorists were exporting their anti-American hatred to the United States, and there was worry among many Americans of potential terrorist

---

[268] Cha, Victor, and Sue Mi Terry. "Assessment of the Singapore Summit." *Center for Strategic and International Studies*, June 12 2018,

[269] Boghani, Priyanka. "The U.S. and North Korea On The Brink: A Timeline." PBS WHYY. Last modified February 28, 2019.

attacks. Previous administrations did nothing to combat the crisis in the Middle East. Under Obama, the ISIS caliphate gained more territory and grew stronger.[270] President Trump took a firm stance. He made it a goal of his administration to destroy ISIS, and he did this by putting generals in place and giving them wider latitude to act quickly and decisively. As a result, the Syrian Democratic Forces, backed by the United States, launched an attack on the ISIS capital of Raqqa, capturing the city on October 17, 2017. Crediting himself with the victory, Trump explained in a radio interview, "[The U.S. victory] had to do with the people I put in and it had to do with rules of engagement."[271]

Alongside the destruction of ISIS, Trump fought for the exit of American troops from the Syrian civil war conflict. He wanted to follow his

---

[270] Tobin, Jonathan S. "Did Trump Beat ISIS?" National Review. Last modified October 19, 2017.

[271] Investor's Business Daily, Editors Of. "Trump Defeats ISIS In Months — After Years Of Excuses From Obama." Investor's Business Daily. Last modified October 17, 2017.

"America first" doctrine and believed American lives should not be taken indiscriminately. He felt little was to be gained in keeping troops in Syria. Since 2011, Syria has been known as a hotbed of contention. The authoritarian regime of Syrian President Bashar al-Assad was challenged by pro-democratic Syrians, who held protests in the streets. Instead of responding to the calls of the protesters, the Syrian government responded with violence. Eventually, opposition militias formed, and a civil war broke out.[272]

Soon after the civil war erupted, Syria's regional and global powers began to split into pro- and anti-al-Assad factions. While Iran and Russia supported al-Assad, countries of the European Union, the United States, and the Arab League wanted him to step down.[273] When it came to military involvement in Syria, the United States, originally did not want to get involved in

---

[272] Encyclopædia Britannica, The Editors Of. "Syrian Civil War." Encyclopædia Britannica. Last modified March 31, 2020.

[273] Ibid.

the conflict. The United States was not willing to spare the lives of American soldiers to fight a civil war.

However, when a sarin gas attack was ordered by the Syrian government on Ghouta in August 2013, President Obama took action, and the United States deployed troops backing the pro-democratic Syrians.[274] While the United States' involvement in Syria was meant to be short-term, it ended up lasting a lot longer, and some Americans were angry that their troops were at risk in an area that they felt did not have strategic importance.

When Trump became president, he made it clear that "we will be coming out of Syria very soon."[275] On October 23, 2019, Trump proclaimed, "After all the blood and treasure America has poured into the deserts of [Syria], I am committed to pursuing a different course, one

---

[274] "Obama's 'Red Line' That Wasn't." Video. YouTube. Posted by The Atlantic, March 16, 2016.

[275] "Trump says Obama could have ended civil war in Syria." Video. YouTube. Posted by CGTN, April 13, 2018.

that leads to victory for America."[276] Although the Syrian civil war still rages on, President Trump has yet again made clear that the United States is not willing to sacrifice American lives in this region.

Despite the conflict in Syria, Iran was an even more pressing issue for the president. Since his run for president, Trump has described Iran as a "rouge regime" because of its destabilizing activities and terrorist threats.[277] Trump disliked the Iran Nuclear Deal, saying that the Obama administration did not go far enough in protecting Americans from terrorist threats.[278] On May 8, 2018, Trump formally withdrew the United States from the Iran nuclear deal by signing a presidential memorandum to begin reinstating

---

[276] "Donald Trump claims victory in Syria." Video. YouTube, posted by Sky News, October 23, 2019.

[277] "Trump Denounces Iran as a 'Rogue Regime.'" *Wall Street Journal*, October, 13, 2017.

[278] "President Donald Trump On The Iran Nuclear Deal." Video. YouTube, posted by CNBC, May 8, 2018.

U.S. economic sanctions on Iran.[279]

On January 3, 2020, Trump ordered a targeted United States airstrike, which killed Iranian military general Qasem Soleimani. Soleimani was a general who despised the United States and was responsible for the deaths of many Americans. President Trump made clear that "Soleimani's hands were drenched in both American and Iranian blood. He should have been terminated years ago."[280] After Trump ordered these actions, Iranians knew the United States was not a country that would back down from a fight.

When one looks at the foreign policy decisions made by both Presidents Polk and Trump, it is clear both men believed in putting America first. Although many foreign policy decisions involve compromise, these presidents would not allow American interests to be threatened by foreign

---

[279] "Trump announces withdrawal from Iran nuclear deal." Video. YouTube, posted by ABC News, May 8, 2018.

[280] "Why did Trump order the killing of Iran's Qassem Suleimani?" Video. YouTube, posted by Guardian News, January 10, 2020.

nations. Throughout their respective tenures as president, both men had a policy agenda of putting America first and protecting the American way of life.

Chapter 15: An Economic Revival

When Polk and Trump took office during their respective presidencies, the United States economy was struggling. Previous administrations had not addressed this issue, and the number of unemployed Americans was on the rise. American prosperity could not be restored if the economic condition of Americans did not improve. During the respective Polk and Trump presidencies, the economy was not just revitalized—it soared.

When Polk presided over the House of Representatives in 1837, America was experiencing an economic depression, resulting in high unemployment rates. Many Jacksonian Democrats had accused President Martin Van Buren of starting the Panic of 1837, even though it was due to President Jackson's policy of eliminating the national bank. When Jackson was president, he vetoed the re-charter of the second national bank. This resulted in state banks receiving government money instead. Consequently, these banks financed wild speculation in federal lands, which resulted in bank failures and panic as depositors lost their savings. In an attempt to remedy the effects of the Panic, Van Buren urged Congress to pass the "Divorce Bill," which aimed to remove the money of the taxpayers from Jackson's state "pet banks" and instead place them in the Independent Treasury. When this measure was presented to Congress, Whigs and some Democrats argued that doing this would worsen the economic depression; however, after an additional round of bank failures in 1839, Congress was prompted to pass the bill in 1840.[281] While the plan seemed economically feasible on paper, the developing United States did not have the modern methods needed to implement it. After Van Buren left office, the Whigs repealed the "Divorce Bill," ending the short-lived Independent Treasury.

Despite Van Buren's skill as a politician, he could not save the country from a major economic collapse. In his defense, nobody could

---

[281] Wilson, Major L. *The Presidency of Martin Van Buren.* Lawrence, KS: University Press of Kansas, 1984. 99, 114.

have saved the United States economy from ruin. America did not have the extensive financial tools it has today; therefore, failure was inevitable. Despite Van Buren's unpopularity, there were some Democrats who still supported him and wanted him to be elected president in 1840. As the *North-Carolina Standard* professed:

> "*Resolved,* that we have unshaken confidence in the ability, virtue, and patriotism of Martin Van Buren, President of the United States, and feel it incumbent on us to use all honorable means to ensure his re-election when the proper period arrives . . . in reference to the Independent Treasury and his strenuous opposition to the United States Bank meets with our hearty approbation."[282]

On December 2, 1845, the first session of the newly elected 29th Congress convened. As the members sat at their desks, they received Polk's

---

[282] Loring, Thomas. "Democratic Republican Meetings." *The North-Carolina Standard* (Raleigh), November 27, 1839.

first annual message to Congress as president. In his usual style, Polk explained the issues the country was facing, his four-point agenda, and how he would implement each of the elements. One of Polk's primary goals was to re-establish the Independent Treasury that the Whigs had destroyed in 1840. To muster congressional support, Polk argued:

"Our experience has shown that when banking corporations have been the keepers of the public money, and have thereby made in effect the Treasury, the Government can have no guarantee that it can command the use of its own money for public purposes. The late Bank of the United States proved to be faithless. The State banks which were afterwards employed were faithless. But a few years ago, with millions of public money in their keeping, the Government was brought almost to bankruptcy and the public credit seriously impaired because of their inability or indisposition to pay on demand to the public creditors in the only currency recognized by the Constitution . . . Entertaining the opinion that 'the separation of the money of the Government from banking institutions is indispensable for the safety of the funds of the Government and the rights of the people,' I recommend to Congress that provision be made by law for such separation, and that a constitutional treasury be created for the safe-keeping of the public money. . . The money of the people should be kept in the Treasury of the people created by law, and be in the custody of agents of the people chosen by themselves according to the forms of the Constitution."[283]

Polk's economic philosophy had always been Jacksonian in nature. Like his mentor, Polk despised monopolistic institutions like the second bank of the United States because it did not act in the interests of the people. With this ideology in mind, Polk understood that Jackson's actions may have led to the Panic of 1837. He also understood that Martin Van Buren had already established an Independent Treasury, and it have proven to worsen the effects of the

---

[283] "Polk's First Annual Message." Address presented at Congress, Washington, DC, December 2, 1845. UVA Miller Center. Last modified April 30, 2020.

financial crisis. The United States economy had changed drastically, however, since 1837. With economic prosperity starting to return, President Polk decided to push for an Independent Treasury, an action that none of his predecessors had been able to accomplish successfully.

While negotiations with Britain regarding the Oregon Territory were underway, Congress discussed Polk's Independent Treasury bill. The bill authorized the president to deposit government funds in treasury vaults, thus ensuring that private banks would not monopolize on taxpayer dollars.[284] When pro-Polk newspapers heard about this measure, they decided to express their support. The *Port-Gibson Herald* proclaimed:

> "Let Congress pass the [Independent Treasury bill] at once if they wish to prove to Bank kings, they cannot rule the nation!"[285]

---

[284] Merry, *Vast Designs,* 273.

[285] Barker, Jacob. "The Independent Treasury." *Port-Gibson Herald* (MS), May 21, 1846.

On April 2, Polk's Independent Treasury bill was passed in the House of Representatives with strong Democratic support and, surprisingly, considerable Whig support. The bill soon went to the Senate, where it was referred to the Finance Committee. After five months, the bill cleared the Finance Committee and passed in the Senate. Four days later, the bill was finalized, and Polk's Independent Treasury came to fruition.[286]

The Independent Treasury bill included three specific measures according to the newspaper The *Kalida Venture*:

> "First, the government will no longer be imposed upon by rapacious bankers. Second, [the Independent Treasury] will always have the public money at command, to pay its debts when due, and third, bankers can no longer speculate . . . off the people's taxes . . ."[287]

---

[286] Merry, *Vast Designs,* 273.

[287] Hall, S. A. "Beauties of a Paper Currency." *The Kalida Venture* (OH), May 14, 1846.

Although Polk's Independent Treasury bill passed Congress with ease, his tariff bill would prove to be more of a challenge.

During the mid-19th century, tariffs were proving to be a contentious issue for many Americans. Northern industrialists and manufacturers supported the passage of tariffs because Americans would buy their products over products imported from Europe. On the other hand, the South opposed tariffs because they had to pay more for manufactured Northern products. The economic backbone of the South rested upon agriculture, not industry. Therefore, although they contributed to the market economy by trading raw materials such as rice and indigo with nations such as Great Britain, the products made from these raw materials were shipped to U.S. seaports in the North where prices were high because of recently passed tariffs. The South did not want to pay these high prices. In 1832, Senator John C. Calhoun and his "Nullies" in South Carolina nullified the Tariff of 1832 because, while it did reduce tariff rates from the previous "Tariff of Abominations" enacted four years prior, prices on foreign goods were still high. South Carolina believed they had the right to nullify the Tariff of 1832 because of the statutes described in the Virginia and Kentucky Resolutions drafted in 1798. These resolutions were based on the Compact Theory of government, which is the idea that since the Union is made up of a compact of states who chose to be in the Union, they have the right to declare any law or ruling from the federal government null and void if it threatens the interests of its citizens.[288] Southerners would continue to use this doctrine not just to nullify tariffs but also to protect the institution of slavery, which was important to the economy of the South.

Although the Compromise Tariff of 1833 ended the nullification crisis, resentment for tariffs carried on into the 1840s. When the Whigs

---

[288] Graber, Mark A. "Compact Theory of the U.S. Constitution." Center for the Study of Federalism. Last modified January 2019.

garnered a majority in both Houses of Congress on March 4, 1841, they drafted a tariff bill that would benefit American manufacturers who needed economic relief after the Panic of 1837. When John Tyler was president, Congress passed the Tariff of 1842. Repealing the terms of the previous Compromise Tariff of 1833, the Tariff of 1842 would benefit the North with high tariff rates of 32% on foreign goods. President Tyler was reluctant to sign the tariff because he was a Southerner and knew how the Southern economy would be affected. Despite Tyler's views, he signed the Tariff of 1842 as a necessity for American manufacturing and much-needed government revenue.[289]

As Polk was emerging onto the national stage as a presidential candidate, he made clear his opposition to protective tariffs but not tariffs that might, in some way, protect specific industries.[290] In other words, Polk believed that tariff rates should be high enough to support government

---

[289] Howe, *What Hath God Wrought,* 593.

[290] Pinheiro, John C. "Walker Tariff of 1846." MillerCenter.org.

revenue, but low enough so that competing economic interests between the North and the South would be minimal. Although many Southern states supported this doctrine, pro-tariff Northern states disapproved of the measure, for a revenue tariff would not provide manufactures with protection from foreign competitors. A state that was hard to persuade over the tariff issue was Pennsylvania, with its coal and iron producers begging for higher rates that would save their industries from bankruptcy. To reassure Pennsylvania, Polk sent a letter to Pennsylvania Governor Francis R. Shunk that stated:

"In my judgement, it is the duty of the government to extend as far as it may be practicable to do so, by its revenue laws and all other means within its power, fair and just protection to all the great interests of the whole Union, embracing agriculture, manufactures, the mechanic arts, along with commerce and navigation."[291]

---

[291] Ford, J. F. "Col. Polk's Letter on the Tariff." *The Ripley Advertiser* (Ripley, MS), July 27, 1844.

Not only did Polk appeal to the coal and iron industries in Pennsylvania with his letter, but he also appealed to the textile industries of the New England states and the traders along the Erie Canal. Polk's promise to protect American industries while enacting a revenue tariff resonated well with the electorate in the North, allowing him to win not just Pennsylvania but also New York. Shortly after Polk's inauguration, a new tariff bill became necessary.

As the Mexican-American War raged on, the federal government urgently required revenue to pay for supplies for the American soldiers in the Southwest. Although the Independent Treasury would provide some revenue, President Polk believed the income would ultimately come from his proposed tariff bill. Before Polk formulated the new tariff, he needed the answer to the following question: What is the fixed rate of a protective tariff? To find the answer, Polk instructed Treasury Secretary Robert Walker to conduct a nationwide survey to find the exact percentage. Before this study was conducted, tariffs throughout American history did not have standardized rates and therefore tended to fluctuate depending on the goods taxed. With this study in mind, President Polk could devise a tariff that had a fixed regulated rate, as this would provide a blueprint for all forthcoming tariff bills.

Using Walker's analysis, Polk drafted the Walker Tariff, which called for "decreased rates at revenue-only levels and a set rate on all goods regardless of value."[292] If this tariff bill were to pass, Walker predicted an increase in customs revenue as a result of increased trade. The measure would also help to negate the rivalry between Great Britain and the United States, for both countries supported free trade policies.[293] Shortly after the bill was drafted, it was sent to Congress, where it was met with divisiveness.

As expected, Southern congressmen and even congressmen from the West supported the Walker Tariff, while Northerner congressman disliked the low rates. In the House of

---

[292] Ibid., "Walker Tariff of 1846"

[293] Howe, *What Hath God Wrought*, 765.

Representatives, Whigs attacked the bill by arguing that it would damage the economy, making the United States unable to finance the war in Mexico. After considerable debate, the House passed the bill 114 to 95. Then, it went to the Senate.[294]

As senators debated the new tariff bill, Polk needed to convince the Northern Democrats of the benefits of his tariff policy. Although Polk was a man of honest convictions, he did tend to bend the truth to achieve his goals. This was clearly the case during the 1844 election, where he proved to be anti-tariff in Southern states and pro-tariff in Northern states. The *Somerset Herald* articulated:

> "In every state where the anti-tariff policy is predominant, or in which the party holds anti-tariff opinions, there Mr. Polk is pressed upon the confidence of the people as an anti-tariff man, which he is. But in states such as Pennsylvania, his claims to confidence and support are urged with equal zeal, on

---

[294] Merry, *Vast Designs*, 274.

the opposite ground, that is to say, because he is a tariffman, and a tariffman equal 'up to the hub.'"[295]

When the voting day for the Walker Tariff came in the Senate, there were arguments along sectional lines, resulting in a tie. To break the deadlock, Polk's vice-president, George Dallas, needed to cast the deciding vote. The Pennsylvanian cast the tie-breaking vote that made the Walker Tariff a reality.

Following the passage of the Walker Tariff, the economy boomed. Along with an increase in free trade, the revenue of the federal government increased from $30 million to $45 million.[296] The funds from the tariff, along with the funds from the Independent Treasury, would allow the United States economy to fund the Mexican-American War. Polk had achieved economic prosperity in the United States, making the American nation more powerful than ever before.

---

[295] Row, Jonathan. "Pennsylvania and the Tariff." *The Somerset Herald* (Somerset, PA), July 28, 1846.

[296] Markham, Jerry W. *A Financial History of the United States*. Armonk, N.Y.: M.E. Sharpe, 2002. 190.

Although Polk's measures contributed to a more robust economy, this effect did not last. There would still be arguments over tariffs, even if there was a standardized rate of taxation, and the country was still prone to economic recessions. During the Civil War, large amounts of gold, silver, and other hard currency would be hoarded with the expectation of increased prices. This led to rampant inflation and a new argument over the use of hard currency. Fast-forwarding to the 20th century, the stock market crash of 1929 and the debt accumulated from World Wars I and II further weakened the previously robust American economy. By the time the 21st century arrived, the 2008 financial crisis would create economic turmoil in America similar in nature to the Panic of 1837. As time went on, the national debt increased. During the Obama administration, $9 trillion was added to the national debt, and currency, not backed with any intrinsic value, was being created on a digital screen. The average American's standard of living was declining.[297] Returning to economic prosperity would require courageous leadership and a person with strong knowledge of the nuances in the American economy. The American people hoped that Donald Trump would provide solutions.

During his 2016 campaign, Trump called for less government involvement in the economy, lowering taxes for the middle class, and enacting tariffs on countries that took advantage of American industries. His call for a revitalized economy was conveyed very simply in the final presidential debate of the 2016 election:

> "Look, our country is stagnant. We've lost our jobs, we've lost our businesses, we're not making [American products] anymore. Our product is pouring in from China, and American factories are shutting down. . . If we could run our country the way I've run my company, we would have a country that [the

---

[297] "Obama economy vs. Trump economy." Video. YouTube. Posted by Fox Business, September 7, 2018.

American people] would be proud of."[298]

Trump's emphasis on the economy appealed to the average working-class American who wanted an improvement in the economy so as to raise their standard of living. When Trump became president, his objective was to deliver on his economic promises.

On April 26, 2017, President Trump revealed a tax plan that would lower the tax rate for corporations and middle-class Americans. The goal for corporations was to lower tax rates to keep corporations from moving overseas and ultimately expand their U.S. operations and hire more American workers to produce goods at home. This measure would cut corporate tax rates from 35% to 15%.[299] For individuals, the tax plan would double the standard deduction, reduce seven tax brackets to three, reduce tax rates for

---

[298] "Third Presidential Debate 2016 | Clinton, Trump on Growing the Economy." Video. YouTube. Posted by ABC News, October 19, 2016.

[299] "Trump unveils massive tax cut plan." Video. YouTube. Posted by ABC News, April 26, 2017.

lower- and middle-class Americans, and repeal the estate tax. When the bill was drafted, it was only one page, and it would have to be voted on in Congress multiple times before the president could sign it. Trump's proposed tax bill was the first step toward economic revitalization.

When the proposed tax bill made it to Congress, Republicans in the House and Senate supported it, although they believed the proposed 15% tax rate was ambitious. Republicans were also concerned about how the government would pay for this tax cut unless it was backed by a new tax on imports. On the other hand, Democrats called the proposal unserious and a giveaway to the rich.[300] Along with Democratic politicians, economists said the tax cut would contribute to a higher budget deficit, greater income inequality, lower healthcare coverage, and higher healthcare costs.[301] Although this commentary was meant to

---

[300] "Congress reacts to Trump's tax plan outline." Video. YouTube. Posted by CBS Evening News, April 26, 2017.

[301] Board, The Editorial. "The Tax Bill That Inequality Created." The New York Times. Last modified December 16, 2017.

dissuade the Republicans from voting for the bill, they remained faithful to their commander in chief. On December 19, 2017, eight months after President Trump proposed the tax legislation, a preliminary version managed to pass through the House. The next day, the tax bill was taken to the Senate for the final vote, where it passed 51–48. On December 22, 2017, Trump signed the tax bill two weeks ahead of its originally scheduled date, offering, as the president said, "tremendous opportunities for businesses, [the American] people, the middle-class, the workers, and corporations, who are going wild over this beyond my expectations."[302]

The Tax Cuts and Jobs Act of 2017 was the formal name given to Trump's tax cut bill, and it did the following:

- Reduced the corporate tax rate from 35% to 21%
- Reduced individual middle-class taxes by, on average, $1,000

---

[302] "President Donald Trump signs Tax Cuts and Jobs Act in Oval Office | ABC News Special Report." Video. YouTube. Posted by ABC News, December 22, 2017.

- Doubled the estate tax exemption to $11.2 million
- On the negative side, the tax bill limited the state and local tax deduction to $10,000[303]

The objectives of this bill were to bring factories and jobs back to the United States from overseas and to put more money into the hands of the American people. To further his objectives of retaining and growing the American workforce, Trump imposed tariffs on steel and aluminum imports in March 2018, leading to a trade war with China. The United States ended up getting revenue from these tariffs, and dying American steel and aluminum plants began operating again. Furthermore, under the Trump administration, the stock market saw impressive gains, with indexes such as the Dow Jones Industrial average rising by over 10,000 points.[304] The unemployment rate also reached an all-time low,

---

[303] Ibid., "Trump signs Tax Cuts"

[304] Jones, Chuck. "Trump's Economic Scorecard: 3 Years In Office." Forbes. Last modified February 10, 2020.

dropping from 9.3 percent to 3.9 percent.[305]

The most profound similarity to recognize between Presidents Polk and Trump as related to the economy is that both men's policies contributed to an economic revival. When each of these presidents entered the Oval Office, the economy was not terrible, but it was also not thriving. Under their administrations, both presidents brought much-needed changes that provided great prosperity and hope to the American populace. With the improvements in the nation's economic condition, the United States became a more powerful, more vibrant nation.

---

[305] Klein, Philip. "Trump's average unemployment rate is the lowest in recorded history." The Washington Examiner. Last modified January 10, 2020.

Chapter 16: Outcry from the Political Establishment

Both Polk and Trump tried to fulfill the promises they had made to their respective constituents. Despite having majorities in both chambers of Congress after the election, members of the party in the minority, as well as some members of their own party, condemned their agendas. These opposing viewpoints resonated with enough voters that when the midterm elections were held, the opposing party would take control of one of the houses of Congress, resulting in more outcry against these presidents' respective political agendas.

The Mexican-American War ignited controversy, as many members of Congress believed the United States had unlawfully encroached on Mexican soil. The Whigs denounced the war because of the slavery issue, which surfaced whenever new territory was acquired. After Polk left office in 1849, Congress ultimately agreed to a new Compromise of 1850 that mandated that California would be a free state. All territories in the Southwest, including New Mexico and Utah, would determine the legal status of slavery through popular sovereignty, the belief that the settlers of a territory, not the federal government should decide. The accomplishment of one of Polk's essential presidential goals, the expansion of American territory, led to disputes among the Democratic and Whig Party members over the institution of slavery, which ultimately led to the American Civil War.

Congress also argued that Polk had abused his power when he declared war on Mexico. Many Whigs argued that President Polk, not Mexico, had started the war. Commenting on Polk's abuse of executive power, Daniel Webster, the patriotic senator from Massachusetts, explained:

"No power but Congress can declare war. . . but what is the value of this constitutional provision, if the President of his own authority may make such

OUTCRY FROM THE POLITICAL ESTABLISHMENT

military movements as must bring on war?"[306]

Alongside this claim, the Whigs argued that Polk was using the war as a political advantage in the next election. Unfortunately for Polk, the war with Mexico did not result in any gains for the Democrats. Some of Polk's Democratic supporters in Congress condemned how Polk had handled the Mexico issue.[307] Although Polk ignored the rhetoric from his critics, he was in for a rude awakening after the midterm congressional elections.

Unlike the midterm elections of today, the election for members of the 30th Congress lasted from August 2, 1846 to November 2, 1847. The results of this election revealed the genuine opposition to Polk as president. In the House of Representatives, the Northern Whigs managed to gain enough seats for a slight majority. Although

---

[306] Webster, Daniel, *Writings and Speeches*, "Public Dinner at Philadelphia," December 2, 1846, (Boston, 1903), IV, 31-32.

[307] Howe, *What Hath God Wrought*, 764.

the Democrats managed to maintain control in the Senate, the balance of power had changed,[308] and although the 30th Congress would not officially convene until December, Polk was concerned, for he did not have the widespread support he needed for the war in Mexico.[309]

On December 6, 1847, the first session of the 30th Congress was about to commence. In his annual message, Polk continued to assert that Mexico had spilled American blood on American soil, and therefore, the United States had the right to instigate war with Mexico. The Whigs, on the other hand, believed that territory should not be taken from Mexico and that the president was being overly aggressive in attacking Mexico because of monies owed by them for damages incurred in the Texas Revolution of 1836. The president also explained that the weak Mexican government could not control its northern territories in the Southwest, and the United States needed to act promptly; otherwise, other nations

---

[308] Holt, *Rise and Fall of the Whig Party*, 238-245.

[309] Howe, *What Hath God Wrought*, 770.

could take the land for themselves.[310] What was the Whigs' response to Polk's claim? As usual, the United States was in the wrong, and Mexico was in the right.

Sixteen days after the 30th Congress had convened, a Whig representing the state of Illinois was about to challenge Polk's argument. This Illinois representative was none other than future President Abraham Lincoln, who, at this point, was just reaching national prominence. Lincoln introduced to his colleagues his "spot" resolutions, which demanded that Polk reveal the exact spot where American blood had been spilled to prove his claims. Despite the Whig majority, the House did not vote in favor of the "spot" resolutions, and the Senate, with its Democratic majority, followed the same action. Shortly after, the Whig-dominated House made it clear that any piece of legislation aimed to raise money for the war or to send more American troops to the Southwest would be voted down. Alongside this measure, a group of radical Whigs

---

[310] Polk, James K., *Presidential Messages*, IV, 532-40.

attempted to pass a motion that aimed to call off the war and bring the American troops home.[311] This measure did not pass.

While congressmen were the most critical group of Polk's Mexican War, literary greats and political satirists who closely aligned themselves with the Whig political establishment also provided their fair share of criticism. One notable example came from James Russell Lowell in his poem "Hosea Biglow," which was part of a more extensive series of poems comprising one book known as *The Biglow Papers*. Written in the dialect of an American yeoman farmer, Lowell wrote:

---

[311] Smith, Justin, *The War with Mexico*, (New York, 1919,) II, 261-63.

> "Ez fer war, I call it murder,–
> There you hev it plain an' flat;
> I don't want to go no furder
> Than my Testyment fer that...
> They may talk o' Freedom's airy
> Tell they'er pupple in the face,–
> It's a grand gret cemetary
> Fer the barthrights of our race;
> They jest want this Californy
> So's to lug new slave-states in
> To abuse ye, an' to scorn ye,
> An' to plunder ye like sin."[312]

Like the Whigs in Congress, Lowell denounced the war with Mexico. Alongside Lowell, authors of the transcendentalist movement also voiced their opposition. In the summer of 1846, Henry David Thoreau, the famous transcendentalist author from Massachusetts, refused to pay his poll tax because the funds procured from the tax would

---

[312] Lowell, James Russell. *Biglow Papers*. Boston: Ams Press, 1969.

support the war with Mexico, which Thoreau despised because he thought Polk was misusing his war powers as president. As punishment for not paying his poll tax, Thoreau spent one night in jail. Two years later, he would publish his real thoughts in his essay "Civil Disobedience," which included the following excerpt:

> "It is not desirable to cultivate a respect for the law, so much as for the right . . . Law never made men a whit more just; and, by means of their respect for it, even the well-disposed are daily made the agents of injustice. A common and natural result of an undue respect for law is, that you may see a file of soldiers . . . marching in admirable order over hill and dale to the wars, against their wills, ay, against their common sense and consciences, which makes it very steep marching indeed, and produces a palpitation of the heart."[313]

The primary purpose of Thoreau's essay was

---

[313] Thoreau, Henry David. *Walden: And, on the Duty of Civil Disobedience*. Waiheke Island: Floating Press, 2008.

to make clear the consequences of President Polk's executive decisions. Thoreau, along with many other literary greats, believed American soldiers were sent out to die in Mexico, all because President Polk wanted to expand the territory of the United States.

Although the Whig Party in Congress was critical of Polk's policies, Polk managed to accomplish his presidential agenda of expanding American territory. He was able to handle the harsh critique of the Whigs successfully; after all, he had been listening to their rhetoric since 1839 when he was Governor of Tennessee. Despite the disagreements, the Treaty of Guadalupe Hidalgo passed, and the Mexican-American War ended. No matter what the Whig Party thought of the eleventh president, one thing was for sure: James K. Polk would never back down from his desire for a stronger United States.

Like President Polk, President Trump lost control of the majority in the House of Representatives after two years in office. This provided challenges to his political agenda; however, like Polk, he had been successful in passing significant portions of his agenda during the first few years of his presidency.

On election day 2016, not only was the president selected, but the entire House of Representatives and one-third of the Senate was up for reelection. On the night that Trump won the presidency, the Republicans gained a majority in the House of Representatives and the Senate. This cleared the way for the Republican Party to enact President Trump's political agenda.[314]

Along with his "Make America Great Again" doctrine, President Trump was called to "drain the swamp" in Washington, D.C. During a campaign rally in Colorado Springs, Trump professed, "If I am elected president, I will push for a constitutional amendment to impose term limits on all members of Congress . . ."[315] Trump

---

[314] Jr., Perry Bacon. "Trump Win, Republican Victories in Congress May Spell Big Changes." NBC News. Last modified November 9, 2016.

[315] "Trump Pushes for Term Limits on Congress Members." Video. YouTube. Posted by Associated Press, October 18, 2016.

supporters praised this idea. Many were tired of the lobbyists and special interest groups turning Washington into a den of corruption. Republican Congressmen such as Ted Cruz, who had argued with Trump on many fronts during the campaign, agreed with the President on this matter, saying:

> "When the framers designed the Constitution, they envisioned citizen legislators who would leave their jobs, businesses, and farms for a period of time; come to Washington, serve the nation, and then go back. We don't have that arrangement today. It is my hope that one of the first things that we'll see Republican majorities in both houses do is take up a constitutional amendment providing term limits, two terms for Senators and three terms for members of the House. . . It's one of the most effective ways to end the corruption in Washington and to 'Drain the Swamp.'"[316]

---

[316] "Ted Cruz: Term limits an effective way to 'drain the swamp.'" Video. YouTube. Posted by Fox News, January 5, 2017.

Unfortunately, this idea did not gain enough Republican votes to pass. Although President Trump had his Republican support in Congress, he also had his detractors.

Throughout his campaign, a small minority of Republican congressmen vowed that they would not support President Trump because of his temperament. For instance, Senator John McCain explained, "There are no excuses for Donald Trump's offensive and demeaning comments."[317] Others disliked the president because of his playboy reputation. Senator Kelly Ayotte from New Hampshire professed, "I cannot and will not support a President who brags about degrading and assaulting women."[318] Although these senators voiced their opinions, their anti-Trump rhetoric was not as fierce as Senator Lindsey Graham's of South Carolina. Graham started to show disfavor towards Trump after comments he made about John McCain, stating that he was not

---

[317] "Republicans in Congress Speak Out Against Trump." Video. YouTube. Posted by Roll Call, October 12, 2016.

[318] Ibid.

a war hero because the enemy had captured him. In one CNN interview, Graham had the following message for Trump:

> "Tell me what you would do about anything. Tell me how you'd solve the immigration problem. Tell me what you'd do with Iran. Articulate a solution to America's problems. Stop disparaging people like Senator McCain, it doesn't elevate you; it gets [the Republican Party] all off in a ditch. Try to realize that you are running for the highest office in the land, the strongest voice in the world, and take the quest more seriously. [Trump's voice] is a loser's voice; I want a winner's voice."[319]

After reading this comment, one would imagine that President Trump and Senator Graham would continuously butt heads, and Trump's policies would not advance. However, over time, Graham started to show a change of heart towards the president. What had begun as

---

[319] "Sen. Lindsey Graham: Donald Trump is a 'jackass.'" Video. YouTube. Posted by CNN, July 20, 2015.

hateful commentary suddenly turned into "I'm going to try to help our president, Donald Trump, be as successful as possible."[320] Why was this the case? Senator Graham answered this question, saying to a *New York Times* reporter, "I've got an opportunity up here working with the president to get some really good outcomes for the country."[321] This newfound relationship between Graham and Trump created a bond of political strength in Congress. Trump could now trust the senator from South Carolina. In usual Trump fashion, Graham candidly remarked, "If you don't like me working with President Trump to make the world a better place, I don't give a shit."[322]

In the first few days of the Trump presidency,

---

[320] "Lindsey Graham's ever-changing tone toward Trump." Video. YouTube. Posted by Washington Post, October 2, 2018.

[321] Leibovich, Mark. "How Lindsey Graham Went From Trump Skeptic to Trump Sidekick." New York Times. Last modified February 25, 2019.

[322] Ibid., "Graham's ever-changing Tone."

the United States Congress was firmly divided among party lines and unwilling to compromise. Although many Republicans had the president's back, Democrats despised him, for they were upset about the 2016 election results. One of Trump's first goals as president was to halt illegal immigration to the United States, under the umbrella of protecting American citizens. Trump hoped Congress would be able to put their political disagreements aside and vote for immigration reform. Unfortunately, Congress was deeply divided over this issue, and Trump's effort to pass immigration legislation failed. Like President Polk, Trump did not wait for Congress to act, however, and instead decided to take action. On September 5, 2017, the Trump administration announced that Deferred Action for Childhood Arrivals (DACA), which was initially passed by President Obama, was no more. Under the program, 800,000 young undocumented immigrants (Dreamers) were brought to the United States to share in the American Dream. Many Democrats feared that legal protections would be taken away from innocent children. After Trump signed an executive order repealing DACA, pressure was put on Congress to enact legislation that would preserve the program's protections before DACA recipients lost their status on March 5, 2018. The ability of Congress to act was about to be tested.

Upon hearing the news of the DACA repeal, Speaker of the House Paul Ryan showed optimism that Congress would be able to come to a compromise:

> "It is my hope that the House and Senate, with the president's leadership, will be able to find consensus on a permanent legislative solution that includes ensuring that those who have done nothing wrong can still contribute as a valued part of this great country."[323]

Senate majority leader Mitch McConnell expressed similar sympathies:

---

[323] Kopan, Tal. "Trump ends DACA but gives Congress window to save it." CNN. Last modified September 5, 2017.

"President Obama wrongly believed he had the authority to rewrite our immigration law. Today's action by President Trump corrects that fundamental mistake. This Congress will continue working on securing our border and ensuring a lawful system of immigration that works."[324]

In a call for bipartisan agreement, the Democrats seemed to remain unamused by Trump's executive action and, as always, attacked the president. "Dreamers' lives are not bargaining chips," Representative Michelle Lujan Grisham proclaimed. "We should not be using them as pawns in furthering a twisted, cruel, and hateful anti-immigrant agenda."[325] House minority leader Nancy Pelosi aired further grievances, calling the repeal "a despicable act of political cowardice."[326]

---

[324] Ibid.

[325] "Trump's DACA decision met with criticism, applause and resolve in Congress." Video. YouTube. Posted by Washington Post, September 6, 2017.

[326] Ibid.

The Republican Party was more optimistic. Republican Congressman Lindsey Graham articulated:

> "From a Republican party point of view, this is a defining moment. We need to create a process to fix a broken immigration system. Starting with the [Dreamers], I think is a good down payment on what will eventually be a comprehensive solution to a broken immigration system."[327]

Finally, wanting to compromise, Senator Graham, along with Dick Durbin, Jeff Flake, and Chuck Schumer, introduced the Dream Act in July 2017. This was a genuinely bipartisan measure "providing a direct road to the United States citizenship for people who are either undocumented, have DACA or temporary protected status (TPS), and who graduate from U.S. high schools and attend college, enter the

---

[327] Ibid.

workforce, or enlist in the military."[328] Another bill called the BRIDGE Act was also proposed. If enacted, the BRIDGE Act would "allow people who are eligible for or who have received work authorization and temporary relief from deportation to continue living in the United States with permission from the federal government."[329] With compromise on immigration finally being met, it was looking as if the new Congress would advance the Trump agenda further. Unfortunately, in the end, the Democratic and Republican Party could not agree on legislation, and this remains an ongoing issue. Ultimately, the DACA program was upheld by the Supreme Court with the proviso that the issue can be revisited provided the administration can provide the lower court with a more robust justification as to why it should end.

---

[328] "DREAM ACT 2017 Summary and Answers to Frequently Asked Questions." National Immigration Law Center. Last modified November 28, 2017.

[329] "FAQ: The BRIDGE Act." National Immigration Law Center. Last modified April 6, 2017.

President Trump was also eager to have his tax bill passed through Congress, as this would stimulate the economy and give working-class Americans a tax cut and corporations more competitive corporate tax rates. The objective was to incentivize corporations to keep more high-paying manufacturing jobs in the United States. While many Republican congressmen were anxious to get this bill passed, Democrats firmly opposed the tax measure. "If the President plans to give a massive tax break to the very wealthy in this country, a plan that will mostly benefit people and businesses like President Trump's, that won't pass muster with we Democrats,"[330] Senate minority leader Chuck Schumer argued. Months went by, and debates ensued between the Republicans, who fought, along with President Trump, to retain and grow manufacturing jobs in the United States while reducing taxes for middle-class Americans, and the Democrats, who reiterated their position that

---

[330] "President Trump's tax reform plan sparks debate." Video. YouTube. Posted by Fox News, April 26, 2017.

the legislation favored the rich.

Perhaps the most powerful debate in the months following the proposal of the tax bill was between Republican Senator Orin Hatch and Democratic Senator Sherrod Brown. "Corporations are sitting on a lot of money right now," Senator Brown proclaimed. "They're sitting on a lot of profits now; I don't see wages going up. So just spare us the bank shots and the sarcasm and the satire, and let's move forward."[331]

As a true defender of American prosperity, Senator Hatch conveyed his message to the Democrats and Senator Brown:

> "Listen, I've honored you by allowing you to spout off here, and what you said was not right. I come from the lower-middle class originally. We didn't have anything! So don't spew that stuff on me. I get a little tired of that crap. And let me just say something: If

---

[331] "Senators get into shouting match over new Republican tax plan." Video. YouTube. Posted by Global News, November 17, 2017.

we've worked together, we could pull this country out of every mess it's in, and we can do a lot of the things that you're talking about too. I think I've got a reputation of having worked together with Democrats!"[332]

Two minutes later, Senator Hatch delivered his final commentary:

"I'm telling you this bull crap that [the Democrats] throw out here really gets old after a while!"[333]

With a heated exchange such as this, one wonders how a tax bill could pass Congress. Congress was just as divided then as it was during James K. Polk's presidency, and it looked as if neither side would come to a compromise. However, just like the 29th Congresses during Polk's presidency, the 115th Congress during the Trump presidency was controlled by the Republicans, and the tax bill passed along party lines. On December 20, 2017, Trump's tax bill

---

[332] Ibid.

[333] Ibid.

passed both houses of Congress, and two days later, it was signed in the Oval Office. "After eight straight years of slow growth and underperformance, America is ready to take off,"[334] Senate majority leader McConnell said after the bill passed.

When President Trump took office, he had the benefit of having a majority in both the House and the Senate. As a result, he was able to pass his tax legislation. He was not successful on the term limit issue or the BRIDGE Act legislation, however, because some members of his own party would not agree to it, and, as a result, it did not have enough votes to pass. However, Trump would soon have an even more difficult road to maneuver because, like President Polk, the midterm elections would create gridlock in the legislature, with little being accomplished except through executive orders.

November 6, 2018 can best be described as a

---

[334] "Senate passes historic GOP tax bill, House to revote." Video. YouTube. Posted by CBS This Morning, December 20, 2017.

night of surprise on both sides of the political aisle. Republicans were hoping to hold their majority in both chambers of Congress to support Trump and his policies. Democratic congressmen, on the other hand, despised Trump and targeted enough House seats hoping for a majority in the House of Representatives.

The morning following the midterm elections, the media reported that Washington was now divided. The Republicans had lost control in the House of Representatives, with the Democrats gaining 28 seats. On the other hand, the Republicans had maintained their control in the Senate, gaining two seats. The American populace was divided, and the Democrats, with the majority in the House of Representatives, would stop at nothing to halt the Trump agenda and investigate the president. "[These results] are about restoring the Constitution's checks and balances to the Trump administration,"[335] House majority leader Nancy Pelosi proclaimed the

---

[335] "Democrats regain the House as record number of women elected to Congress." Video. YouTube. Posted by ABC News, November 7, 2018.

night the election results were broadcast.

On January 3, 2019, the 116th Congress convened, rekindling a worry in Trump that President Polk had felt 170 years earlier. President Trump no longer had the majority in both chambers of Congress, and therefore, the advancement of the Trump agenda would be challenged and derailed by the Democrats in the House. Furthermore, Trump would become the subject of many investigations proposed by the House Democrats, ranging from obstruction of justice to Russian collusion in the 2016 election. The House Democrats, out of their hatred for the president, even impeached him on the charges of "abuse of power" and "obstruction of Congress." Trump, however, was not impeached on any legal statutes, unlike former President Clinton. In the Senate, the Republicans acquitted Trump on both charges. Republican and Democratic interests have never been more divided in Washington. The question now remains: Will both sides compromise to advance Trump's agenda? Only time will tell, but the American people are not hopeful.

During the Polk's and Trump's respective presidencies, both men received their fair share of criticism from Congress. Even when they had a majority in both chambers of Congress, some members of their own party opposed their political agenda. After their respective midterm congressional elections, both presidents lost the majority in the House of Representatives. This political setback made it more difficult for them to continue working on their agendas.

Chapter 17: Benefits for the Least Noticeable

A measure of success of any presidential agenda lies in the benefits bestowed upon the American citizenry. The political agendas of both Presidents Polk and Trump included benefits for the least noticeable, the people who had been ignored by the government and whose standard of living was being affected by it. Presidents Polk and Trump would make sure that the voices of the ignored were heard.

Following the passage of the Walker Tariff of 1846, the Northern industrialists, plagued initially by the effects of the Panic of 1837, gained massive benefits. The heavy importation of goods from both the American and European side not only fully remedied the effects of the previous financial panic, but also provided Northern industries with the funds needed to continue their businesses, resulting in few workers losing their jobs. While the industrialists achieved prosperity, another group that became even more prosperous was American farmers.

Shortly after the Walker Tariff passed Congress, the *Daily Union* published an excerpt written in the *Norwich News* explaining the methodology that farmers would follow to increase their profits:

"The fairer we make our tariff for other nations, the greater will be our own exportation–that is, the more they will want to buy of us... It is as it would be with two neighbors–one from necessity, perhaps, may for a time pursue a course of conduct, which is of great indirect, or perhaps direct benefit to the other. Should the other, having the power at command to do so without injury to himself, reciprocate these favors, the result may be a closer bond of union between them, and the creation of still greater mutual benefit."[336]

The same year that the Walker Tariff was passed, Great Britain repealed its Corn Laws, a set of protective tariffs on foodstuffs and grain imported from the United States and other foreign nations. With the Corn Laws in effect,

---

[336] Ritchie, Thomas. "'Protection' to the Farmer." *The Daily Union* (Washington, DC), September 12, 1846.

farmers were not making profits abroad because the British were not willing to pay high prices for American grain. Now that both countries had repealed their tariffs, American farmers were able to gain profits and did not have to foreclose on their farms.

Even though farmers were becoming prosperous because of President Polk, many of them despised him. The war with Mexico had painted a bad image of the president in the minds of farmers who resided in the northwestern United States. Recall the poem "Hosea Biglow," written in the dialect of a yeoman farmer, that described the war with Mexico initiated by President Polk as murder. To assuage the feelings of the farmers, the *Staunton Spectator* wrote:

". . . the rise in the price of American produce in foreign markets, is consequent upon the policy of the [Polk] administration. . ... let the farmers of this country, who are happily, getting a good price for their produce, rest in the belief that ordinary events have turned the market in their favor, rather than to suppose that [President Polk] has produced misery abroad, that they might profit by demands thus strangely created."[337]

Due to the Polk administration's actions, American farmers were able to increase their wealth. Remembering the philosophies of his mentor, Andrew Jackson, James K. Polk knew that every policy he enacted needed to benefit the Americans whose cries were continually being neglected by the federal government in Washington.

Although farmers prospered during Polk's presidency, this did not last long. Shortly after Polk left office, farmers were neglected and thus returned to the days of minimal profits. Their situation grew increasingly worse during the panic of 1857, when N. H. Wolfe and Company, the oldest flour and grain company in New York City, failed. When the Civil War broke out, farmers reluctantly left their farms and fought for either the Union or the Confederacy. Although other farmers supplied rations to soldiers, they

---

[337] Harper, Kenton. "Great News for the Farmer." *Staunton Spectator* (Staunton, VA.), February 11, 1847.

did not make the same amount that they did during the time of President Polk. Countless administrations would neglect the plea of the farmers, yet they would be reassured when Donald Trump became their president.

On January 8, 2018, President Trump attended a farmers' convention at the American Farm Bureau Federation in Nashville, Tennessee; he was the first president to do this in more than 25 years. After some cheerful banter, he explained the importance of the family farmer as follows:

"We know that our nation was founded by farmers. Our independence was won by farmers. Our continent was tamed by farmers. Our armies have been fed by farmers and made of farmers. Throughout our history, farmers have always, always, always, led the way. . . The men and women in this room come from different backgrounds, but each of you carries the same title: American farmer."[338]

---

[338] "President Trump addresses farmers conference." Video. YouTube. Posted by CBS News, January 8, 2018.

Trump understands the importance of farmers and saw to it that they receive the credit they deserve. On December 20, 2018, roughly a year after he signed his tax cut legislation, he signed the Agriculture Improvement Act. With this legislation, more than $400 billion was provided for farmers and ranchers in the form of agriculture subsidies, conservation programs, and food aid.[339] Before the signing of what was called the "farm bill," American farmers had seen their net income drop by half. With the farm bill implemented, farmers would be able to receive loans from subsidy and insurance programs, improving their economic condition.[340] Although this was a crucial first step, China had imposed tariffs on soybean imports, resulting in many farmers losing income. As an advocate for the American farmer, President Trump could not ignore this attack. The passage of tariffs on

---

[339] "Watch Live: President Donald Trump Signs Farm Bill Amid Impending Shutdown | NBC News." Video. YouTube. Posted by NBC News, December 20, 2018.

[340] "What's in the House's $867 billion farm bill?" Video. YouTube. Posted by PBS NewsHour, December 12, 2018.

Chinese goods was bringing in government revenue and punishing China for damages they inflicted on American industries. On May 23, 2019, President Trump announced that $16 billion would be used as relief aid to farmers who had been affected by the lack of purchases from China due to the tariff war.[341]

In addition to legislation benefiting farmers, President Trump has signed legislation that provides benefits for our veterans who have proudly served our country. Six months before signing the farm bill, Trump signed a piece of legislation that would give veterans the medical attention they need as soon as possible. Previous administrations forced veterans to wait an unacceptable length of time for medical care. Now, they have the opportunity to go to a doctor of their choice if they feel they did not receive the

---

[341] "President Donald Trump Gives $16 Billion To Farmers: 'Good Time To Be A Farmer'| NBC News NO." Video. YouTube. Posted by NBC News, May 23, 2019.

care they deserved in a timely manner.[342] Alongside veterans, the majority of middle-class Americans for years did not have access to affordable healthcare. President Trump vowed to reduce healthcare costs and make programs such as Medicare more affordable. He has signed countless executive orders aimed at protecting and improving healthcare coverage. Unfortunately, however, there has been no recent legislation passed by Congress to reduce healthcare costs.

During the respective presidencies of Polk and Trump, both men provided aid and benefits to groups of people who the government had for many years ignored. In most cases, these were also the same constituents who had helped elect them. President Trump's farm bill appealed to farmers in the Midwest who had voted for him in 2016. Trump also passed veteran healthcare reform legislation because he has compassion for veterans. Some critics would say he took these

---

[342] Marshall, Dianne. "TRUMP'S VETERAN'S ADMINISTRATION REFORMS." The Marshall Report. Last modified June 6, 2018.

legislative actions to appeal to his base. Despite this cynicism from his detractors, it should not be forgotten that Trump is a supporter of the common people whom previous administrations have neglected. There is an old adage: "Actions speak louder than words." President Trump has proven by his actions that he has compassion for the common man.

Many seasoned politicians had to spin their narrative to win. President Polk acted this way towards states such as Pennsylvania, saying that he would support a protectionist tariff in the state while also saying he opposed it in the southern states. Because President Trump is not a politician but a businessman, his approach is more direct. He tells it like it is. He does not care what other people think of him. He stays true to his policy and beliefs, and he cares about the least noticeable and those left behind. In the end, both presidents cared about the plight of the neglected common man.

Chapter 18: A National Rebirth

As a result of the policies and agendas, both Polk and Trump were able to enact, in their presidencies, a renewed spirit of hope associated with putting America first took hold. America became stronger economically. Politically, however, the two parties were more divided than ever before over the political agendas promulgated by both of these presidents. Although the end of President Trump's term in office is still unknown, both he and Polk would leave knowing that their leadership styles and policies led to a national rebirth of patriotism and putting America's interests first.

Looking back at his administrative policies, Polk was content with the progress he had made. With the signing of the Treaty of Guadalupe Hidalgo, Polk had acquired the entire American Southwest from Mexico, as well as Oregon two years earlier. By the end of Polk's term, the map of the United States that every American knows today was nearly complete (missing only Alaska and Hawaii). The only part that still needed to be acquired was a small sliver of land between New Mexico and Arizona. In 1853, this territory would be bought from Mexico for $10 million, thereby completing the acquirement of all of the lower forty-eight states. Furthermore, the passage of the Walker Tariff and the re-establishment of the Independent Treasury provided the government revenue for the Mexican-American War and contributed to a more robust American economy.

James K. Polk did not see any point in running for re-election after completing his agenda. He believed he had fulfilled his role, saying to his ardent supporter and friend, Gideon Pillow:

> "I shall retire at the close of my term with the satisfaction of believing I have rendered my country some service."[343]

Based on his impressive presidential accomplishments, Polk not only provided an invaluable service to his country, but he also

---

[343] Ibid., "The Correspondence of James K. Polk"

offered a model of commitment for future presidents to follow.

In the last days of the Polk administration, a divided Congress debated the government structure in the newly acquired territories. While Polk had hoped this debate would be smooth and effortless, it proved not to be. Although America had achieved its Manifest Destiny, the country had become more divided on the issue of slavery. Even though the Missouri Compromise, with its north latitude line at 36° 30', was in effect, it was beginning to lose force and did not have the same impact as it did during the 1820s and 1830s. Despite the divisiveness, Congress was able to pass a bill establishing a territorial government in Oregon. The Oregon Bill was later sent to President Polk for signing, and with that signature, Oregon, with its population of pioneers, was given a state government.[344] Meanwhile, the newly formed states in the Southwest, including New Mexico and California, did not have bills establishing

---

[344] Merry, Vast Designs, 461.

territorial governments. Ultimately under the Compromise of 1850, California would be a free state, and New Mexico would rely on its own citizens to decide on the issue of slavery.

On March 5, 1849, President-elect Zachary Taylor, the nominee from the Whig Party, was about to become the twelfth president of the United States. Old Rough and Ready, the general who had led the United States to victory in the Mexican-American War, was about to take Polk's place. Taylor was escorted to the Capitol's east portico, where Polk had delivered his patriotic inaugural address four years prior.

In comparison to Polk's inaugural address, Taylor's was rather simplistic and did not call for major political goals. President Taylor's primary objective was to heal a divided nation. With a smooth transition of power in place, James and Sarah Polk boarded a steamboat en route to their newly purchased Nashville plantation, which the former president would name "Polk Place."

Throughout his life, the eleventh president was never of robust health; instead, he was weak and feeble. Although these ailments did not affect

Polk during his presidency, they did affect him shortly afterward. While on the boat ride from Washington D.C. to Nashville, Polk began suffering from severe diarrhea and fatigue. When he arrived in Nashville, he seemed to be recovering, though he was still not well. Accepting that the end was near, the former president completely embraced Christ for the first time in his life, hoping the Almighty would send him to heaven's golden gate in the sky. On June 15, 1849 political underdog James K. Polk died at the age of 53.[345]

Some 170 years later, America would experience its second political underdog in the form of Donald J. Trump. Although Trump is still the President of the United States at the time this book is being written, the policies he has enacted thus far have contributed to a similar rebirth of patriotism. The president's "America first" stance regarding immigration and foreign policy has ensured the protection of the American way of life. Policies including the commencement of a 2000-mile-long border wall along the U.S.-

---

[345] McCormac, *Polk*, 721.

Mexico border has already reduced the number of illegal immigrants entering the United States. It is anticipated that by the end of 2020, 500 miles of the wall will be complete. Early in his presidency, Trump already made it clear to foreign rogue nations such as North Korea and Iran that while he is willing to discuss areas of common interest, the United States will retaliate militarily if threatened. Within six months of taking office, Trump's policy on ISIS led to their complete defeat. With regard to America's involvement in the Middle East, the president has pulled most of the American troops out of Syria, and the administration is currently trying to negotiate a peace treaty with Afghanistan to remove those who remain. The president's policy is to not take sides in unwinnable regional civil wars. The objective is to free up money for domestic needs. America's involvement in the Middle East has already cost it $7 trillion. With regard to China, Trump has been clear that the current economic arrangement, in which the United States runs a huge trade deficit of $500 billion, cannot continue. He has backed this up with a tariff war and a subsequent Phase 1 deal on trade. His administration has also renegotiated NAFTA to reduce the trade deficit with Canada and Mexico.

As part of his domestic policy, President Trump signed into law his tax-cut bill designed to lower tax rates for the middle-class and reduce corporate tax rates in the United States to make them more competitive with foreign countries. With the passage of this came historically low unemployment rates and booming American industries. Trump also cared about the Americans who had been regularly neglected by the United States government in Washington. Legislation such as the farm bill and the VA reform bill provided American farmers and veterans the benefits they deserve for the services they provide to this nation. Although Donald Trump's presidential story is not complete, one can make this claim: President Trump's common man and America first ideals have contributed to an economically stronger and safer nation, albeit a divided one.

Under the direction of Presidents Polk and

Trump, the nation reached a new level of hope, patriotism, and economic prosperity. On election day, the fate of the country was in the hands of the populace, who did not disappoint. If Clay had won the election of 1844 and Clinton the election of 2016, things might have been different. Would America be as safe, and would the economy be as strong? To ignite this change to patriotism and an America first mentality, it took the leadership of two men. Men who experienced hardship and criticism. Men who achieved success despite instances of failure. Men who had temperaments centered around self-determination and resilience. Men who will always be remembered as America's shining set of Political Underdogs: James Knox Polk and Donald John Trump.

Conclusion: Making America Great Again

The story of America's political underdogs has come to an end. Who could have imagined the plethora of similarities between a president elected in 1844 and a president elected in 2016? While there have been other articles that compare James K. Polk and Donald Trump, this is one of the first comprehensive works on the subject.

In an attempt to make parallels between these two men, one must consider both the positive and the negative. In their early childhoods, both men were raised by their families to acquire the values of resilience, self-determination, and grit needed for the land's highest office. As both men progressed into their adolescent years, they further refined these characteristics, as evidenced in the way they approached their educational careers. The respective mentors of these men reinforced these characteristics, as they taught them never to compromise on ideological issues.

Shifting the focus to the electoral scene, one can find a striking similarity between the campaign strategies of both candidates. Polk and Trump advocated for the average citizen by promising that they would address the issues that would benefit them. Although both presidents lost their majority in the House after two years in office, both men still managed to sign legislation and in the first two years of their presidencies to honor their commitments. In addition, Donald Trump continues to address the issues important to the country through executive orders. The electoral outcomes of both presidents also reveal a parallel that is an equally important central premise of this work. Both Polk and Trump were not expected to win their respective elections. The American elite and their politically biased media assumed that the experienced, well-known, and professional establishment politicians would ascend to the presidential office. Yet, James K. Polk and Donald J. Trump disproved this notion. The experiences of both men throughout their young and adult lives gave them the leadership qualities necessary to run the country. Although both candidates received harsh critique from the opposing party and even from some of their own establishment party members, they did not shy away from their ambitions, resulting in policies that not only strengthened America but also revitalized it.

Although both presidents contributed to the revitalization of the country, one might argue that they also contributed to the strong divisions among the United States' political parties and their supporting citizenry. One must acknowledge, however, the positive as well as the negative when it comes to both men. After the respective elections of Polk and Trump, the nation became firmly divided. In the case of Polk, the nation became sectionally divided after the accomplishment of the Manifest Destiny doctrine. Congress continued to debate on the practice of slavery during the 1850s, and, though a compromise was brokered, the rivalry between the North and the South continued. Eventually, the American Civil War, the bloodiest war in American history, would break out.

One might also say that a Trump presidency could result in the rise of a second American Civil War. Since 2016, the Democratic Party and their media supporters have viciously attacked the president regarding his political agenda and his temperament. Some would say the extreme liberal wing of the Democratic Party have even gone to the extreme measure of abandoning the Constitution, criticizing those media outlets and corporations who do not censure a conservative point of view. The conservative wing of the Republican Party continues to this day to fight against this oppression. Over time, the divisions between Liberals and Conservatives might become so high that they lead to violence and even a second American Civil War. One cannot predict when or if this event will occur; however, we cannot dismiss this possibility. Never forget the old adage: History repeats itself, and only the players change.

While the economic prosperity of the American nation was renewed, it unfortunately did not last. After Polk left office, the divisions between the North and South led to the Civil War, which negatively affected the Southern economy. Although Trump is still in office at the time of the writing of this book, the booming economy of the first three years of his presidency is on a steep decline. The COVID-19 epidemic has forced the lockdown of the American economy and ended America's economic revival. As the economy reopens in a slow and systematic matter, President Trump must once again install hope into the American people during this time of crisis. One could only imagine what President Polk would have done if he had to lead the American people through a Pandemic such as COVID-19.

Alongside the policies and state of the Union of the two presidents, a special note must be made regarding the presidents' political parties. James K. Polk was a Jacksonian Democrat from Tennessee. Donald J. Trump is a Republican, a member of the party that, under Abraham Lincoln, fought to abolish slavery through the adoption of the Thirteenth Amendment. How could a presidential party parallel be made between these men when they were members of different political parties? The answer to this question requires an understanding of an essential similarity between the Democratic Party of the Jacksonian era and the modern Republican Party: Removing the issue of slavery, which was decided by the outcome of the Civil War and the passage of the Thirteenth Amendment. The Jacksonian Democrats of Polk's America and the Republican Party of Trump's America both advocate and support the needs of the common man electorate. This political ideology between the two parties of yesterday (the Whigs and the Democrats) and those of today makes the two presidential parties similar.

When it comes to describing any president and their executive actions, praise and criticism are used interchangeably, depending on what party the individual supports. However, Polk's and Trump's respective stories of accession to the presidency offer a moral lesson that resonates with many. The moral that an underdog can, through perseverance and hard work, overcome adversity and become victorious. James K. Polk and Donald J. Trump were not expected to live in the executive mansion. The opposing political party establishment believed they would prevail and stopped at nothing to damage the two candidates' reputations, almost costing them their shots at Commander in Chief. No matter how harsh the rhetoric from the opposition was, both presidents looked towards fulfilling their ambitions. The American elitist establishment and their media partners did not portray these men in a positive manner. They despised their presence and hoped and prayed they would not have to succumb to men who they believed were unqualified and would lead the nation down a dark road. In the ordinary course of events, one would have expected both candidates to throw in the towel and drop out of the presidential race. Many would have argued it was not worth the cost. But, if there is one ideal both men held at the center of their respective moral compasses, it is the importance of never backing down from conflict, no matter the circumstances. During President Trump's first Inaugural Ball, Frank Sinatra's song "My Way" was played. As the lyrics were sung, the stories of Polk's and Trump's rises to the presidency were retold:

MAKING AMERICA GREAT AGAIN

"Regrets, I've had a few
But then again, too few to mention
I did what I had to do
And saw it through without exemption

I planned each charted course
Each careful step along the byway
And more, much more than this
I did it my way

Yes, there were times, I'm sure you knew
When I bit off more than I could chew
But through it all, when there was doubt
I ate it up and spit it out
I faced it all and I stood tall
And did it my way."[346]

It was at this moment that American history would grace each of these men with not only the title of political "Dark Horse" winners but a title that exemplifies the true meaning of American perseverance: Political Underdogs.

---

[346] "President Trump's Inaugural First Dance." Video. YouTube. Posted by Wall Street Journal, January 23, 2017

Acknowledgments

There were many people involved in the creation of this work. I would like to start by thanking my parents Anne Marie Amigues and George Stephen Bojko for supporting me in this project from the very beginning. Also, I cannot thank my fourth-grade teacher, Miss Laura Ann Hood, enough for the comments she offered and her inputs into this book. She inspired me, during my formative and adolescent years, to succeed. Furthermore, I would like to thank the small number of students who agreed to read several chapters of my manuscript during their busy school schedules.

Notably, my Christian faith was of immense importance during the writing of this book. I believe it was Jesus who gave me the strength to continue writing, even into the early morning and late evening. It was Jesus who gave me the gift of knowledge and the passion for American history necessary to write this book.

I wrote this book because the Lord Jesus Christ, in His infinite wisdom, implanted the idea for this work in my mind. With that being said, I dedicate this book in His name.

About the Author:

Alexandre G. Bojko is a dual French-American citizen who moved to the United States from Paris, France in 2011. Currently a Junior in high school, he has tutored students taking Advanced Placement United States History. He has helped countless students receive top scores through the reinforcement of skills such as art and document analysis. Alongside his passion of American history, he is actively involved in the hobby of Numismatics and is a 2019 graduate of the Numismatic Diploma Program, a series of courses offered by the American Numismatic Association.

Made in the USA
Monee, IL
29 October 2020